Kiyo-
Thanks, always,

Bill

Middle-aged Sons and the Meaning of Work

Research in Clinical Psychology, No. 16

Peter E. Nathan, Series Editor

Professor and Chairman
Department of Clinical Psychology
Rutgers, the State University of New Jersey

Other Titles in This Series

No. 8   *The Divorce Experience of Working and
        Middle Class Women*   Toni L'Hommedieu

No. 9   *Climbing the Ladder of Success in Highheels:
        Backgrounds of Professional Women*   Jill A. Steinberg

No. 10 *Work and Marriage: The Two-Profession
        Couple*   Roslyn K. Malmaud

No. 11 *Families of Gifted Children*   Dewey G. Cornell

No. 12 *The Legacy of the Holocaust:
        Psychohistorical Themes in the
        Second Generation*   Robert M. Prince

No. 13 *The First Pregnancy: An
        Integrating Principle in
        Female Psychology*   Jellemieke C. Hees-Stauthamer

No. 14 *Growing Up in the James
        Family: Henry James, Sr., as
        Son and Father*   Katherine Weissbourd

No. 15 *Mothers and Children Facing Divorce*   Tracy Barr Grossman

Middle-aged Sons and the Meaning of Work

by
Richard L. Ochberg

 U·M·I Research Press

Ann Arbor, Michigan

Produced and distributed by
UMI Research Press
an imprint of
University Microfilms, Inc.
Ann Arbor, Michigan 48106

Library of Congress Cataloging in Publication Data

Ochberg, Richard L., 1950-
Middle-aged sons and the meaning of work.

(Research in clinical psychology ; no. 16)
Revision of the author's thesis (Ph.D.)—University
of Michigan, 1983.
Bibliography: p.
Includes index.
1. Work—Psychological aspects—Case studies.
3. Middle aged men—Psychology—Case studies. 3. Middle
aged men—Interviews. I. Title. II. Series.
BF481.033 1987   158.7   86-30709
ISBN 0-8357-1779-8 (alk. paper)

For my father, who taught me to write

Contents

Acknowledgments   *ix*

Part One: The Meaning of Careers

1 The Problem of Work and Identity   *3*

2 How the Men Were Studied   *13*

Part Two: The Dispassionateness of Work

3 On Being Part of the Problem   *23*

4 Nothing Personal   *33*

5 Public Lives and Private Motives   *49*

Part Three: The Trajectory of Careers

6 The Man No One Could Ignore   *57*

7 The Man Who Could Not Stop   *71*

8 An Unambitious Man   *83*

Part Four: Stories Men Tell

9 Family Legends   *99*

10 Why the Uncle Died   *101*

11   A Risky Life   *119*

Part Five: Conclusion

12   The Theater of Careers   *135*

13   Theory as Cultural Criticism   *147*

Bibliography   *153*

Index   *155*

Acknowledgments

The ideas presented in this book reflect a collaborative rumination that I have been fortunate to share with friends, colleagues, and advisors at the University of Michigan and at Yale. The large vision comes from George Rosenwald, whose suggestions are by now so interwoven with my own that I cannot possibly credit them in individual citations. In particular, I owe him the guiding idea of this study: that research should restore shared, unacknowledged problems to public debate. More by example than by explicit theory, George also taught the precarious balance between honoring individual life stories, and moving beyond case portraiture to large, and skeptical, social theory.

Howie Silberstrum heard most of these cases in highly abbreviated and incoherent form, and usually managed to explain them to me. Bob Green, Jeff Evans, and Meg Turner have been my consultants and good friends. Lynne Gressett, Pat Green, and Tina Malcolmson heard infinite, minutely altered variations of these chapters with uncalled-for patience and encouragement. I owe these people a large part of what I understand, and thanks for helping me survive graduate school and the limbo of postdoctorship long enough to write it.

Many of the ideas presented here were first suggested in conversations with Ed Bordin, Barnaby Barratt, John Kotrie, John Mohr, Mark Schneider, and Tod Sloan. Thanks to Bill McKeachie, Frithjof Bergmann, and Bill Cave for their support; to Beth Shinn, who was always unofficially on the committee; and to Jack Safit for the last chapter.

Finally, there are the subjects themselves, who gave their time and emotional energy to these long, intrusive interviews: I owe them my deepest thanks. In order to protect their privacy I have changed their names, locations, and some details about their lives.

Part One

The Meaning of Careers

1

The Problem of Work and Identity

This is a study of how men invest themselves in their work. It offers an interpretation of work's meaning, based on the nuances of phrase in which men describe their careers. To balance what will soon be my microscopic focus, let me begin with what seem to me the largest questions about careers and the lives they embody.

How do men make their lives count? How do they come to feel that life has coherence, worth, purpose? Very largely, the answer is something like this: We each invest ourselves in various commitments. Family is one, perhaps the most important; for most men work is at least second. It is through these commitments that we define who we are and what we value. We live through the medium of what D. J. Levinson (1978) calls "life structures."

A life structure is in its essence a composite. On one side, it is a vehicle for our most personal cares and hopes. For many men, the initial choice of career represents an idealized fantasy of who one is or might become. S. D. Osherson, in a study of men who changed careers in middle age (1980), remarks, "In general, the young adulthood career and marital choices of our group all contained, at their core, a wish to remake or redefine themselves in the mold of a more perfect image. This image is an idealization of the parental figures of their childhood and adolescence" (p. 53).

In a similar vein, Levinson describes what he calls the Dream, an imaginary ideal of what a career might come to be: "In its primordial form, the Dream is a vague sense of self-in-adult-world. It has the quality of a vision, an imagined possibility that generates excitement and vitality. At the start it is poorly articulated and only tenuously connected to reality" (p. 91).

At the same time work cannot be only a private fantasy. It is a public performance, conducted according to social rules and evaluated by shared standards. If the initial choice of work is infused with fantasy, it soon becomes the medium in which those dreams are enacted and judged. Levinson's description of the Dream continues, "Whatever the nature of his Dream, a young man has the developmental task of giving it greater definition and finding ways to live it out" (p. 91). Work becomes perhaps the primary vehicle of psychosocial identity.

We may think of careers, then, as a kind of performance in which private aspirations and public expectations are jointly represented. There is a second way in which careers are double-sided. Not only are they social and individual, they are also both self-expressive and self-denying. Levinson, in a discussion of midlife crisis, notes that every career choice imposes its own limits. If the career grants expression to some aspects of a man's personality, it inevitably demands that he set aside others.

> Why do we go through this painful process? Why should a crisis so often be our lot at mid-life?... Partly because no life structure can permit the living out of all aspects of the self.... In making a choice I select one option and reject many others.... In the Mid-life transition these neglected parts of the self urgently seek expression.... A man hears the voice of an identity prematurely rejected; of a love lost or not pursued; of a valued interest or relationship given up in acquiescence to parental or other authority, of an internal figure who wants to be an athlete or nomad or artist. (Levinson 1978, 200)

Levinson's explanation focuses upon the inherent limits of any choice, laying responsibility for limitation at the door of external constraint. We hope to be many things, Levinson suggests; it is the exasperating finiteness of reality that abbreviates us. His description is accurate, but there is more to be said. Not only does every commitment impose certain limits; from a psychodynamic perspective every choice acts to deny (and, very indirectly, reveal) motives that are intolerable to conscious acknowledgment.

Osherson describes the initial career choice as an attempt to bring to life a perfected ideal, a "wished-for self." This idea of a perfected self-representation goes back to Freud's 1923 account of the ego-ideal. The ego-ideal is not simply an image of what one most admires in oneself, or of what one most wishes to become. It also repudiates what one finds most frightening or distasteful in oneself. The ego-ideal is enlisted in the struggle against repressed desire. The balance is never certain, nor satisfying. As much as it grants expression to favored images of self, this sort of self-idealization is a form of self-denial, always threatened by upheaval.

There is a relationship between these two aspects of the career's double-sidedness, between the way that it is social and individual, self-expressive and self-denying. What belongs to the arena of social behavior and what men are most eager to believe about themselves form an alliance. A career becomes the vehicle of a man's public life. The word "public" captures both sides of this idea. Careers are "public" both in that they are social performances and in that they render visible the part of themselves men are willing to acknowledge. By contrast, what men do not express in their work is relegated to "privacy." At the very least, men deny that these private hopes and fears influence how they conduct their careers. Perhaps, some of them say, they allow themselves to express these private sentiments in some other sphere of life: at home, or with friends. But even this is not certain. What men cannot acknowledge to be part of the meaning of their careers they often cannot admit to be part of their experience anywhere.

This alliance beween social conduct and the idealized image of self depends upon a congruence of values. The way career culture expects men to behave—in order to be effective on the job—is largely what men prefer to believe about themselves for their own psychic comfort. It is always dangerous to generalize too sweepingly, but in broad terms the agreement consists in this: Both the culture of work and the dominant code of masculinity expect men to be emotionally detached, impartial, and aggressive (ideally their aggression should at least appear impersonal). By contrast, both career culture and men themselves become uncomfortable when men express their attachment to each other, or their vulnerability.

Since the demands of careers and men's individual preferences are in such substantial agreement, we might expect men's performance at work to be stable—perhaps not attractive, perhaps not expressive, but at least reliable. But here we come to a problem. Because idealized self-representations exclude so much of who we are, they are inherently unstable. Osherson describes the limits of the idealized work choice, and its potential for collapse.

> There are several reasons why the wished-for self expressed in these choices contained the seeds of later loss. 1. These patterns of self-definition were not flexible, nurturant, confident senses of who one is, but rather a rigid, defensive standard admitting of no compromises. 2. The wished-for self is exclusionary, exiling or suppressing parts of who one is. 3. The wished-for self is actually ambivalently held.... The wished-for self incorporates the person's negative and hostile feelings about the idealized father. 4. Finally, since the choices take into account only part of who the person is, [they] are often based on only limited knowledge of their field.... This makes it even more unlikely that the wished-for self will occur. (Osherson 1980, 55–57)

In this passage, Osherson points to the tension underlying idealization. The consequence is that careers, which embody this idealization, contain the potential for going off course. A career choice reflects not only a man's conscious desires but also, in some disguised fashion, his unconscious impulses and his preferred style of keeping them under wraps. That is, the career is as conflictual as he is. It makes little sense to speak of such a career choice as a solution. It is more an enactment of a problem. (For a discussion of career choice in terms of its congruence with both drive and characteristic defense mechanisms see Bordin's work of 1943.)

How well a career satisfies any individual depends on the balance of repression and satisfaction—including disguised satisfaction of disavowed motives—it affords. This balance is likely to be upset by day-to-day events and by developments throughout life. The compromise is in principle dynamic. It is not like fitting a peg into its proper slot; it is more like compressing an unruly spring into a container and wondering how long it will stay.

The Culture of Upper-Middle-Class Careers

I have been speaking about the culture of careers as if it were some unitary thing. Clearly it is not. There are substantial differences between the social environments of corporate managers, salesmen, store owners and professors, to mention the occupations of only some of the men in this study. Further, within each occupation there is room for individual variation. There would certainly be merit in exploring a single business culture in detail. Nevertheless, it is striking how similar are the occupational concerns these men describe.

This book concentrates on two principal themes that emerge with singular repetitiveness in the descriptions these men give of work: emphasis on emotional detachment and preoccupation with career advancement. This book describes the relationship between these two cultural themes and certain recurrent patterns of psychodynamically motivated self-denial. It does not argue that career culture is created by psychodynamic motives: that would be absurdly reductionistic. But it does argue that an alliance exists between certain culturally favored forms of behavior and certain familiar patterns of self-expression—and self-denial. It attempts to describe the reasons and the costs—private and public—of this self-estranging alliance.

Personal Relations in the Culture of Work

The culture of upper-middle-class careers demands that men retain their detachment. This general prescription takes several specific forms. First, men must remain emotionally detached from whatever task engages them. Don, a psychologist, described to me an incident from his days as a Navy chaplain during the Vietnam War. The commander of the ship brought him a man who was considered a security risk. So strong were the sailor's moral qualms about the war, the commander feared he might not do his job. Don eventually left the Navy when his own discomfort with Vietnam grew intolerable. But even today, looking back on the incident, he speaks with asperity. The large machine of the ship requires that every human cog turn smoothly. Personal concerns cannot be allowed to interfere with the smooth operation of a large organization.

Detachment also governs men's relations with each other. Obviously men do have strong feelings toward their colleagues; however, they are expected— and expect themselves—to set those feelings aside in work relationships. Ken, who manages a factory and prides himself on his personal touch with subordinates, nevertheless explains: "If someone is not doing a good job it is your obligation to terminate him. It is twice as hard if you are close. You are better off being aloof if you are going to be a terminator. . . . I have never fired anyone who . . . hadn't received direct warning, 'When you leave, you will leave that minute. Pack up your stuff and be gone.'"

Ken's description illustrates a recurrent problem of work relationships. How much room is there for favoritism? Officially, the work code is rigorously impartial. Sutton (1956), borrowing Parsons' terminology, describes what he calls the American Business Creed:

> The classical model is universalistic in its very fundamentals. It represents a system in which individuals gain or lose according to an impersonal gauge of their performance. What individuals get in the system is not dependent either (a) on the opinions which others may hold of them, or (b) on the sense of responsible concern they may have for others or others for them. . . . The system allegedly puts every individual up against the same impersonal conditions and in this sense treats them fairly. (Sutton 1956, 260-61)

In actual practice, however, this impartiality is more difficult. Inevitably, alliances based on mutual affection spring up. Cultivating these alliances is a large part of business success.

Bob, another industrial manufacturer, was in the midst of going bankrupt during the time I interviewed him. He exemplified the contradictory expectations of work culture. On the one hand, he described in corner grocery images the million-dollar-a-year business his family owns: "Business is interpersonal dealings. For twenty-five years my father called the head of the steel company. 'Hi Irv, I need 10,000 pounds of so and so next week, and have you any so and so today?' It is like a fruit peddler, for crying out loud." On the other hand, Bob recognized that any appeal to his creditors could not be based on the claims of loyalty, but only on the most matter-of-fact pragmatism. "I told him, 'I make a high quality part for you, which means no rejections for you, either. Now we are in financial trouble, and the corporate head seems to prefer to give the job to someone else, instead of helping me out. If you could speak to him . . . I will improve my financial position and be better able to help you in the future.' I said, 'Help us if you want to. If not, try someone else, and maybe they will be as good, and maybe not.'"

The problem is not simply that work culture demands detachment, while men's own preferences would lead them to be more personal. The ambiguity runs through the heart of work culture itself. Officially, the code demands the impartiality Sutton describes. Unofficially but just as insistently, good business practice demands that men establish alliances. I mean this in more than the ordinary sense that men who work together should get along. Beyond this, there is an understanding that good fellowship is the grease that makes the machinery of sales, administration or service run smoothly. Good fellowship is as much a product to be sold as boots and carburetors.

This point has been made several times in descriptions of postindustrial character. D. Riesman (1950), for example, traces the rise of the "outer-directed" personality to the institutionalization of enterprise, arguing that modern society has moved beyond the heroic age of individual achievement. The production of wealth is no longer left to the imagination and vigor of individuals. Instead, it has become routinized by large corporations whose operation is increasingly detached from individual initiative. In this new pattern, the sturdy self-reliance of the nineteenth century is replaced by a character type who orients himself through interpersonal sensitivity. R. Sennett (1978), whose description parallels Riesman's at many points, laments the modern pressure toward superficial intimacy at the cost of a more profound narcissism.

If work culture insists on conviviality, the very calculation behind it renders all friendliness suspect. Where intimacy is known to be a tool of salesmanship it cannot be trusted:

> Salesmen assume a cheery enthusiasm and friendliness; the clerks in women's stores behave with saccharine familiarity.... Assumed friendliness has an even more obvious significance in the problem of initiating business relationships.... Outgoing "friendliness" in this sense has obvious functional importance in a dynamic progressive economy.... It also gives rise to considerable strain.... Where narrow self-oriented relationships are clothed in the forms of more intimate relationships, suspicions about sincerity can hardly be avoided. (Sutton 1956, 341–42)

The men I interviewed commented frequently on this strain in their own experience. Ken, for example, described his aversion to the personal politics of salesmanship. "I hate the goddamn game [of golf]. Why should I put myself into such frustration chasing some stupid white ball around because some guy I am selling to happens to enjoy that kind of masochistic game?" During sales meetings, Ken prefers to have his sales representative handle the interpersonal diplomacy while he deals with impersonal business. "The representative can handle all the small-talk crap back and forth. And I'll go in and handle the business part of it."

The strain imposed by this calculated fellowship gives rise to a number of attempted solutions. Some men repudiate the whole business. They avow an interpersonal ethic whose watchwords are tough, fair, impersonal, unemotional and pragmatic. Bob was one of these. The style, however, is difficult to pursue. The practice of work does not really allow most men a retreat from personalism. Bob tried, but as we will hear, he went bankrupt. He now thinks he may have paid insufficient attention to the diplomacy of sales.

Another possibility is for men to assert that personal relationships are really the most attractive aspects of work. Several of the men I interviewed made a claim of this sort. There is an inevitable deception here: anyone who seriously believed this and tried to make work into an arena of genuine relatedness would inevitably be frustrated. Several of my informants found themselves in this position. These men, who could not distinguish the pretense of affection from its reality, were destined to break their own hearts over and over.

A third possibility is to enjoy the camaraderie of work within its own careful boundaries. This is the solution that the work culture itself encourages, yet it is a difficult solution, requiring a careful balance of genuine engagement and ruthless disinterest. Ken was the model of this type. He explained, "I am not saying that the people who work for me, that it is a stand-offish relationship ... but there is still a natural barrier that prevents it from going from the sixty-fifth percentile to the ninety-eighth—whatever. It just can't be; it has to be guarded. It can't become a friendship because I am in a control position."

Ken is an enormously successful man, but I suspect some readers may find the model he offers unpalatable. The dilemma this study describes is that what works is not appealing, and what appeals does not work.

The Imperative of Career Advancement

The culture of work strongly encourages the expectation that a man's career will describe a rising trajectory. C. Sofer's description of a British corporation is representative: "Success in a career, as judged by the person himself and his colleagues, is closely connected with age. Careers are age-graded. Certain positions or grades in organizations and professions are characteristically reached by a particular age. One's career is 'working out' if one has 'made the grade' at the appropriate age" (Sofer 1970, 53).

In some settings the emphasis on career advancement takes precedence over all other work interests. Salary and the intrinsic interestingness of specific jobs are considered less important than the job's position in a sequence of expected advancement. "Some jobs, furthermore, lost their meaning and became, instead, stepping-stones on the path to upper management. Indsco's people got the message: Be promoted or perish. You are not really successful, or you do not mean much to the company, unless you get the chance to move on. Thus jobs and job categories were evaluated in terms of their advancement prospects, quite apart from job content or actual grade level and salary" (Kanter 1977, 130–31).

This emphasis on career advancement is not at all limited to corporate culture: self-employed businessmen and professionals are equal subscribers. Even factory workers, whose hope of advancement is realistically minimal, espouse the rhetoric of getting ahead (Chinoy 1952).

Not only are careers expected to advance overall, there may be expectations for qualitative changes at different age-linked points. Levinson suggests that a man expects himself to achieve some special degree of autonomy and authority in his forties. The task is to "become one's own man." Al, a real estate salesman who is debating moving on to some larger company or starting his own firm, remarked, "I have done this thing [selling real estate]; proved that I am awfully good at it. If I take myself seriously it is time to move on to the next thing. . . . I am living with the belief that I am supposed to be challenged at all times . . . that the real goal in life is some kind of development and challenge."

There are connections between career advancement and the impersonality of work culture. Not only does the pressure to advance lead to lack of interest in the actual content of the job, it requires an ability to detach oneself quickly from colleagues. W. E. Henry, in a passage that begins to sketch the relation between career culture and psychodynamic themes, remarks:

> In general the mobile and successful executive looks to his superiors with a feeling of personal attachment and tends to identify himself with them. . . . On the other hand, he looks to his subordinates in a detached and impersonal way, seeing them as "doers of work" rather than as people. . . . It is as though he viewed his subordinates as representatives of things he has left behind, both factually and emotionally. . . . He cannot afford to become personally identified or emotionally involved with the past . . . In a sense the successful executive is a "man who has left home." He feels and acts as though he were on his own, as though his emotional ties and obligations to his parents were severed. (Henry 1949)

Henry's description of the businessman who "acts as though he were on his own, as though his emotional ties to his parents were severed" hints at a psychological connection between career advancement and detachment. Henry notes that if the executive's mobility is blocked, he is likely to suffer psychosomatic distress. There is a strong suggestion here that mobility may serve to deny anxieties, or intolerable wishes, associated with leaving home. But Henry does not offer an opinion as to what this distress may represent. If, as he implies, the cultural imperatives toward detachment and mobility are related to psychodynamic themes, the exact nature of that relationship is left uncertain. This is the territory of this study.

Violations and Restorations of the Code

Always granting some room for iconoclasm, and some tolerance for variation within the cultural prescription itself, most men conduct their careers within the broad outlines of this formula. Social relationships at work are necessarily valued, but principally as a matter of smooth accommodation to readily interchangeable partners, or as a means to tactical advantage. This, at least, is the cultural mandate, and it is largely how men explain themselves.

But this code of behavior (and self-understanding) cannot possibly accommodate the range of feelings men actually have toward each other. Periodically something else intrudes: a desire to become someone's special favorite or to have one's own diffident advances of affection recognized; fears of humiliation; and fantasies of vengeance. The occasions for these lapses vary. Often these men, still at forty seeing themselves as the younger generation, look toward an older man for special attention: Al, for example, wanted to be made a partner by his boss. Sometimes the play of generations is reversed: Ken's story turns on his fury at a protégé whom he had selected as a favorite, but who misused Ken's friendship for personal gain. Sometimes men choose much more diffuse targets as the objects of their sentiment. Mike, a small store owner, imagined himself running an old-time family business. He sought the affection of a whole small-town community that he hoped would patronize his establishment for its personal atmosphere, and ignore the lower-priced shopping center down the road. When these men felt themselves rejected—as, eventually, each of them did—they reacted violently. Al dreamed of setting off on his own (and in competition with his ex-employer), Ken demoted his protégé ruthlessly, Mike launched a sale, designed to shock the community, that ended with his own bankruptcy. In each case the personal note behind the business decision was unmistakable.

All of these men shied away from the personal motives behind their decisions. Each explained his behavior as if it were governed only by the impersonal logic of business—often straining logic to do so. Each of these men had briefly let down his guard—and been discovered—and then restored the temporarily discomfitted illusion of detachment by redoubling his allegiance to the official code. So, Ken, humiliated by his protégé's rejection, explained what seemed to be vengeance in terms of company policy. "People expect this situation to be resolved in a legitimate manner.... [The old president] was a waffling type; I'd like to change that. This guy happens to be part of that image. It isn't strictly personal. If [the employees] are going to make a contribution, the company is going to have to make some sort of contribution too, and do it in a forthright, honest manner."

These moments of temporary lapse and subsequent restoration constitute my point of departure. In them, I suggest, can be read a connection between the code of upper-middle-class careers and psychodynamically motivated self-estrangement. The career code provides a culturally mandated formula of denial. It serves as a neurotic defense. In the moments that it fails we hear what men cannot allow themselves to acknowledge: their sentimentality and their fear of self-diminishment. These men's exaggerated, rigid, and often destructive pursuit of this culture's values becomes intelligible as an attempt to preserve a defense against their own discomfiture.

Plan of the Book

This book is built around seven case histories. Every case argues a similar point, though from a slightly different angle. Each presents a man who describes some current feature of his work life. In several cases there are dramatic, focal events: Ken wrestling control of the family company from his brother; Bob losing to bankruptcy the company he had inherited from his father; Mike launching an ill-considered sale and losing a fortune. In other cases there are no immediate, dramatic shifts of fortune, but rather men talking about their ongoing worries. Lew and Al, each in his own way having achieved more success than he can hope to repeat, contemplate quitting their jobs and starting over, while Ben describes feeling trapped and bored. Don, recently promoted, describes his fear of stress.

Each man presents his concerns in the most ordinary, factual terms. And yet, as they describe more of their lives and we notice other incidents described in repetitious imagery, we begin to see that their immediate concerns are parts of a series. Don, for example, worries about losing emotional distance. There is nothing unusual here: any manager might say as much. But Don couches his concern in a striking phrase: he does not want "to become part of the problem," and this phrase, repeated back through his life history, leads eventually to a very particular set of fratricidal fantasies.

The seven cases are grouped into three sections. In the first, Don and Ken describe the dispassionateness of work. Each of them wants to feel close to his colleagues, yet they both fear—for somewhat different reasons—that losing personal distance may be dangerous. In a notably imperfect solution, each adopts a self-explanation provided by the culture of careers. They say, "I am only acting out a role." The second section deals with career advancement. Al, Mike, and Ben each describe the meaning of ambition and its symbolic rendition in career trajectory. Here too the issue is attachment to colleagues (or students, or customers). Aggressive ambition provides these men a defense against the self-diminishment they experience when they feel rejected. The third section, entitled "Stories Men Tell," presents a reversal of the usual psychodynamic logic of careerism. The two men in this section, Bob and Lew, do not use their careers to change themselves. Instead, each tells a story of his father's career (Lew, in a complicated identification, performs this story in his own life) that changes the meaning of both the fathers' career and the man's own career. These stories are told—in Lew's case performed—within the cultural conventions of dispassionateness and trajectory.

Before we examine these cases, however, the next chapter presents a brief description and rationale of how I went about interviewing these men and interpreting their stories.

2

How the Men Were Studied

This study explores the idea that men's careers serve as symbolic vehicles of self-representation and attempted self-perfection. In order to investigate this idea, I have compared the imagery men use to describe their careers with the images with which they describe other formative experiences and recurrent life themes. In this chapter I describe how the study was conducted, and why, and attempt to answer certain possible objections.

I contacted by telephone fourteen men who were recommended to me by friends. The criteria were simply that the potential informant be about forty years old and that he have been engaged in some career for at least five years. Eleven men consented to be interviewed. The exceptions were a prominent local journalist who feared he could not be adequately disguised, a store owner who heard me out suspiciously and declined, and a lawyer who pleaded no time. Of the eleven, I report seven cases here.

Each man was interviewed five times, for an average of one hour each time. Many interviews were considerably longer, so that for some men the total time was nearly ten hours. Interviews were conducted at either their home or mine, or once or twice at a business office. All interviews were tape recorded and transcribed.

I generally began, after a brief introduction, by asking an informant to tell me about his work. What did he do, what about his work did he like, how did he get interested in it? For the first half hour or so I deliberately limited the conversation to the sort of things men talk about on the train. Sometime in the second half of the first hour I began asking about connections between work and other experience—high school, grade school, family, friends—in part out of interest in the information and in part to see how willing the man was to explore more personal questions with me. Subsequent interviews pushed increasingly toward more personal issues.

The panel of men described here are all at least middle-class; one is quite wealthy. This was a deliberate choice. Although virtually all men judge themselves partly in terms of what they have achieved in their vocation, not all work lends itself to the identification of self and career that Levinson describes in his idea of the Dream, and Osherson in the wished-for self. There is a difference between the sort of work that engages one's aspirations and the sort that offers a pay-check but little room for self-expression. The line between these two may be difficult to predict. There are laborers who take pride in their effort, while the most disenchanted man in this study was a college professor. Still, it seemed that the best chance of finding men who had re-created themselves through their work would be among those who pursued at least middle-class careers. (In assessing the developmental problems that several of his working-class subjects faced, Levinson remarked that they never seem to have developed a vocational Dream.) The group presented here includes a store owner, a salesman, two men who direct small manufacturing companies, two who hold middle-level posts in public administration, and the professor. In light of the sober assessments to come, this stacking of the deck toward vocationally favored men bears emphasis.

A second decision concerned the men's ages. One obvious possibility would have been to interview young men just setting out on their careers. At this stage of life the relation between self and vocation—or at least, between a wished-for self and the Dream of a vocation—might be most readily articulated. However, I was interested not only in the ways careers represent the self, but the possibility that careers may alter these self-conceptions. In particular, I wanted to explore whether men might use their work as a sort of symbolic theater whose effect would be to transform their own internal dialogue with the parents of their childhoods. To this end it seemed useful to interview men who had already established themselves in their careers. Men who had already accomplished something might demonstrate not only what careers incorporate of self-idealizing daydreams, but how those self-idealizations are transformed by concrete success, or lack of it.

The men of this study are all in their late thirties or early forties. They have all been engaged in some work for at least ten years, though most of them have changed jobs several times along the way. This in itself does not seem a serious problem. As I will show, changing from one job to another is itself a salient feature of what these men mean by "career." Another reason for choosing men of this age is that the forties have frequently been described as a time of midlife crisis: a time when men question their careers and, indeed, their entire lives. It seems possible that in these moments of turmoil men might be engaged in asking themselves much the same questions that I would ask them.

In fairness, I should point out that some investigators would be skeptical of this reason. Despite all the popular attention that midlife crisis has received, hard evidence remains uncertain. Farrell and Rosenberg describe the popular conception of midlife crisis:

> There is a growing body of work in popular culture that provides us with a set of hypotheses about middle age. Its approach seems to involve upheaval.... This crisis is not always experienced consciously, but may lead to alterations in behavior or attitudes on several

fronts, or escape into psychosomatic illness, alcoholism, and psychiatric disturbance. Although extreme reactions such as divorce or "chucking it all" to run off with the younger woman may be relatively rare behaviorally, they are portrayed as common thematic concerns and salient fantasy material for the middle aged male. The themes of rebellion, rebirth and erotic release are heavily emphasized. Those who have succeeded within the system find themselves nonetheless bitterly disappointed, while those who have failed tend to be miserable about both their striving and its meager results. (Farrell and Rosenberg 1981)

The authors note, however, that there is little systematic evidence that such a crisis is a part of average experience.

Levinson believes that at about age forty men enter a period of transition, which leads them to reorganize their lives. He suggests that this is a universal aspect of adult development. However, his samples are comparatively small and, by his own account, the transformation he has in mind may be subtle. A. Campbell, speaking to Levinson's thesis remarks:

When we look at men at this age [40–45] in the national samples, we find no indication that their feelings of affect or satisfaction with life or the domains of life are in any way unique to that five year period.... No doubt points of transition similar to those Levinson describes occur in the lives of most men and women in American society, but they are either not linked as closely to specific ages as he believes or they do not create the kind of affective or evaluative response that would be recorded by the kind of questions our surveys ask. (Campbell 1981, 181)

B. L. Neugarten (1976) comments that, far from describing themselves as distressed, the middle-aged men and women in her studies describe themselves as the "command generation."

On the other side, Farrell and Rosenberg (1981) present evidence that midlife crises may be much more widespread than studies based on self-report discover. They find indication of a widely experienced crisis that is also widely denied. They describe patterns of disappointment masked by the superficial appearance of well-being or authoritarian denial.

In a study of forty-year-old men, L. Tamir (1982) describes more specifically the relation between work and life satisfaction. She finds that satisfaction with work itself does not decline at midlife. If anything, men describe themselves as being more competent and having more clout than at younger ages. However, work satisfaction seems to contribute less to overall life satisfaction for forty-year-olds than for younger men. The sphere of work shrinks in subjective importance.

This finding is particularly relevant to this study. If career is a vehicle of self-expression (and, simultaneously, self-denial) through young adulthood, and if careers shrink in importance during midlife, we should expect forty to be a time of psychological turmoil. Not only must men find new vehicles of self-expression, those aspects of personality that the career served to deny should re-emerge. They should be evident, if not in direct self-report, in the indirect forms of projected fantasy and memory.

I am not certain that the men I interviewed were more troubled at this time of their lives than at other points. For whatever combination of developmentally predictable reasons and lucky accident, this study did capture several men at what seemed to be significant turning points in their careers. Ken was wrestling control of the family company from his brother, Bob was trying to save his family's company from bankruptcy, and Mike had tried to expand his business and had succeeded in losing it. Rumination about career change figured large in the thoughts of several other men. Lew and Al, each of whom had succeeded well beyond his own expectations, were considering striking off in new directions. Ben spoke of feeling trapped. Of these men, only Bob ever used the term "midlife crisis," and the crisis he had in mind was financial, not one of spiritual malaise. He, like the others, experienced his troubles and choices in the most practical of terms. But if these men themselves did not spontaneously reflect upon what their careers had meant to them, the fact that they were now changing directions provides us the occasion for this interrogation.

At this point the skeptical reader may enter an objection. We may grant that middle age has its predictable crises of self-doubt. But is it really reasonable to view the cares of middle-aged men from the perspective of their late-adolescent (or worse yet, childhood) fantasies? Neugarten (1968), for example, speaks skeptically of what she terms "childomorphic" approaches to the study of adulthood. Henry (1949) describes successful executives as those who appear to have severed their ties to childhood. G. E. Vaillant describes the sense his middle-aged informants had of leaving behind their parents, and even the mentors of early adulthood:

> However, while acknowledging that their mentors were often "father figures," the men took care to differentiate these mentors of adulthood from their real fathers. In more than ninety-five percent of cases, fathers were either cited as negative examples or were mentioned as people who were not influences.... One man closed his description of his mentor with an epitaph: "I was the featured speaker at his retirement." Other men assured me that the models of their young adulthood now had feet of clay. (Vaillant 1977, 218–19)

It is certainly not my intention to describe adult life as merely a continuation of infantile character. Interpretations of midlife crisis that discover in it nothing but the reenactment of the Oedipus complex beg to be disbelieved. All theories lend themselves to vulgarization.

On the other hand, it is possible to view any significant life event as evoking responses from several different periods in a subject's life. Rosenberg and Farrell (1976) describe the mixture of realistic concerns for aging parents and the resurfacing of aggressive fantasy that may occur in middle age:

The personal sense of vulnerability and decline is sharply juxtaposed with the unfolding shift in status. It occurs in a context where the middle-aged male is being thrust into the symbolic position of patriarchal leader. His own father is nearing death and is being progressively stripped of the roles and status which had reflected his dominance.... This displacement of the father presumably evokes stress and internal conflict. While supplanting or out-achieving the father may have been a central project for the maturing adult, his actual ascendency is over a now weakened and sympathetic figure. Guilt and depression would intermingle with any potential elation.

The interpretive perspective that views current life events as, in some measure, infused with the echoes of earlier experience contains a further assumption. If my own outlook is not by this point evident, let me take this occasion to declare it. I interpret these cases on the assumption that some portions of subjective experience may become cut off from the normal process of maturation. These meanings, which are repressed, live on as unconscious scenes. Life comes to be lived on two tracks: one that shares the consensual world of adulthood and another that experiences adulthood in terms of unrecognized, infantile understandings and motives. This split-off, internally alienated part of personality colors every experience. At some moments, when events fall too close to home, the infantile interpretation becomes particularly strong. At those moments a man's behavior can seem irrational—sometimes even to himself—and emotion frighteningly intense. It is in this sense that I bring psychoanalytic interpretation to the study of adult careers. It is compatible with both Neugarten's admonition that adulthood is more than infantile repetition and the psychodynamic thesis that adult choice may disavow repressed, childhood desire.

So, for example, I read Vaillant's description somewhat skeptically. It does not seem to me surprising that adults emphasize their independence from childhood attachments. Attachments are broken consciously. I suspect, however, that there remain unconscious meanings which color even these men's experience. If these meanings are unconscious, we obviously cannot imagine that we will discover them in these men's self-reports. On the other hand, the repressed sometimes betrays itself in the voice of denial. Vaillant's description lends itself to the interpretation that his subjects are protesting too much. To mention a father as a negative example is not at all to deny his importance. To emphasize that one's father was not an influence only invites the skeptical question, "Who asked?" Finally, to note of a mentor, "I spoke at his retirement," does not suggest that the speaker has outgrown the conflict, but that he remains keenly aware of the rivalry of generations. I have much the same reaction to Henry's descriptions. When I hear that a man gives the appearance of severing his ties to childhood, but that he develops psychosomatic symptoms when his forward progress is blocked, I am led to wonder what defensive function is being served by the self-idealizing image of "getting ahead."

The prospect of discovering reasons that go beyond those my informants themselves offer raises a different methodological objection. Once again, a skeptical reader may interrupt: "All that you propose may be true, but how can anyone else be sure?" The question is reasonable, and I will try to answer it. But it may first be useful to address a particular methodological commitment that, I believe, lies behind the question: the assumption that only a particular type of data and verification can ever be considered admissible evidence.

All research must provide some basis for assessing its credibility. In the large majority of sociological and psychological studies, that test is based ultimately on the apparent objectivity of the data. Data appears objective when it is self-evident, when any observor can be counted upon to say, for example, "Yes, this is an instance of ambition (or self-deception, or whatever is being studied)." C. Taylor (1971), in "Interpretation and the Sciences of Man," remarks,

> The attempt is to reconstruct knowledge in such a way that there is no need to make further appeal to readings or judgments which cannot be checked further. [The] basic building block of knowledge on this view is the impression, or sense-datum, a unit of information which is not the deliverance of a judgment, which has by definition no element in it of reading or interpretation, which is a brute datum. The highest ambition would be to build our knowledge from such building blocks. (p. 29)

However plausible this ambition may be for the bulk of social science— and it is Taylor's contention that it is largely implausible—it quite evidently cannot do justice to the project I describe here. The point of this study is to undermine the appearance of objectivity: to show, for example, that when Ken claims to behave in the dispassionate interests of his employees he is simultaneously acting to disguise from himself his own emotion. This project is committed from the beginning to the idea that words and actions have multiple meanings, that some of these meanings may not be self-evident, that in fact, the purpose of acting or speaking in a particular way may be to disavow meanings that are subjectively intolerable. Where meanings are as ambiguous as they will be in this study, an audience of readers can be expected to disagree about any interpretation. What then are we to do? Here I return to Taylor, who describes nicely both the procedure of interpretation and its ultimate recalcitrance to "objectivity."

> How does one know that [an] interpretation is correct? Presumably because it makes sense of the original text: what was strange, mystifying, puzzling, contradictory is no longer so. . . . [But] what if someone does not "see" the adequacy of our interpretation, does not accept our reading? We try to show him how it makes sense of the original non- or partial sense. But for him to follow us he must read the original language as we do, he must recognize these expressions as puzzling in a certain way, and hence be looking for a solution

to our problem. If he does not, what can we do? The answer, it would seem, can only be more of the same. We have to show him through the reading of other expressions why this expression must be read in the way we propose. But success here requires that he follow us in these other readings, and so on, it would seem, potentially forever. We cannot escape an ultimate appeal to a common understanding of the expression, of the "language" involved. This is one way of trying to express what has been called the "hermeneutical circle." (pp. 28–29)

If interpretation can never break out of the circle of readings—if it can never find ultimate anchor in self-evident data—it can, nevertheless, become pursuasive within its own code of evidence. Taylor indicates the direction from which that evidence must be sought: the widening circle of mutually confirming readings. I can now describe, somewhat more concretely, what I make of men's stories.

In each case I begin with a man who describes a current concern about his work life in the most ordinary, objective terms. Don laments the stress of a new job, Ken describes the tactics of a corporate coup, Bob worries about his father's health if the business goes bankrupt.

Interpretation starts when we begin to doubt the story as we first hear it. Sometimes doubt is inspired by the sheer illogic of the behavior itself. Mike, for example, says he persisted in a disastrous sale because he needed to reassure customers that he was not going out of business. In fact, the sale ruined him, and so forced the very outcome he claimed he was trying to avoid.

But incidents of this sort are rare. The men described here are not fools; for the most part, the explanations they offer are plausible. In most cases our attention is captured by something less blatant than Mike's example: a gradual realization that what a man says about the events that concern him are part of a long-standing theme, a kind of obsessive rumination that runs through his life history. Bob, for example, worries that if the family business does go bankrupt his father may die. The thought is certainly plausible; his father created the business, and has poured his life into it. Yet in the course of describing how the family business grew, Bob recounts an older piece of family history, in which an uncle, a partner in the firm, "died of a broken heart." The father's feared death now appears part of a longer history, in which the lethal power of this family corporation is a recurrent motif.

The second stage of interpretation uncovers the hidden significance of current experience. In practice this means tracing the imagery of current self-report back to childhood. Bob's memories of childhood focus on his long-standing, passive struggle to be free of his father's interference; a struggle that ended, reluctantly, when Bob himself joined the family business. In the light of this longer history, Bob's attachment to the business seems equivocal, and his apparent solicitude toward his father takes on the shadow of less admissible desires.

Each case proceeds similarly. We start with a puzzle—a piece of extravagant behavior, a peculiar preoccupation, a chronic dissatisfaction. Each time we work backward from the appearance of businesslike detachment to the troubling personal sentiment it conceals.

The final movement of interpretation reverses direction. Here I try to show how the individual borrows from the code of work, especially its themes of career trajectory and detachment, in order to explain away his own private preoccupation. This is the point at which individual portraiture returns to the level of culture.

A last word about interpretation may be necessary. While sociologists and some psychologists may find any discussion of suppressed childhood meaning unwarrantedly speculative, clinicians may object that the interpretations offered here do not go deep enough. For the most part I point out connections between how men describe their lives at forty and other descriptions of their teenage years or late childhood. As psychodynamic theory goes, these connections point to developmentally late experience and self-understanding that may be painful to acknowledge but not really unconscious. My aim, however, is not to uncover the foundations of self-representations, but simply to show that there is something more to these stories than men comfortably acknowledge. To this end even superficial excavation is sufficient, and perhaps more widely credible.

Part Two

The Dispassionateness of Work

3

On Being Part of the Problem

The reader of these cases may find himself puzzled by their apparent one-sidedness. Why am I so intent on depicting the troubles of adult life? Have I stumbled on an unusually disenchanted group of informants? These men do not seem extraordinarily damaged. Do I mean to say that all adulthood is an unhappy affair? Surely there is more to midlife than its celebrated crisis.

The reason lies in what it is that we wish to discover. Of course there is more to adult life than disillusionment. If this study focuses on the barely expressed anxieties of these ordinary men, it is only to see what they, as average citizens of the work culture, can show us of its deceptive language. I mention this as a general comment, but also by way of introduction to Don, our first case. If anything, Don is a happier man than most. Still, there are strains in his life whose meaning—framed by the misexplanations of career culture—escapes him. This is what I will attempt to explain.

Don is forty-five, married, and the father of a thirteen-year-old boy and an eleven-year-old girl. For the past ten years Don has been a psychologist with the Jackson State Penitentiary. His original training, however, was for the ministry. He served as a military chaplain between 1965 and 1970, and completed his training in counseling psychology in 1973, after leaving the Navy.

Two years ago the prison began a massive reorganization. As a result, Don became the director of two projects: an alcoholism treatment center and a halfway house for men newly released from the prison. Both programs are running successfully, yet there remain the inevitable strains of reorganization.

D:	The center is starting something and creating it at the same time.
RO:	That is a mixed sort of blessing.
D:	It is mostly a non-blessing as far as I am concerned. I have been through that with the center before; ideologically I disagree with it. I'm the sort of person who has to plan through a thing to some degree before I do it.

The fact that Don is uncomfortable making up the rules as he goes is not remarkable. Some administrators fly by intuition, others by the codebook. Of interest to us is the larger meaning of this anxiety for Don and the way he uses the culture of work to misexplain himself.

The first point to notice is Don's acute discomfort with hectic disorganization, and the care he takes to avoid becoming disconcerted. Don prepares carefully for each day. Two hours before leaving his house in the morning, he considers his goals for the day and the amount of time that each should consume. Without this sort of planning, he explains, work would take over his life. Should he feel overly stressed during the day he will pause to meditate or leave the building for a walk. Once he goes home, he attempts to put work entirely out of mind. This can be difficult, since at times he is still on call for emergencies.

> When I come home I don't want the rest of the world to intrude. Right now I am on back-up. The way I deal with that is to focus on what is here. If the phone rings, then I'll deal with it. But if I don't deny, project, compartmentalize to some degree, then every time the phone rings I flinch and I can't give my attention to the kids doing their homework, whatever.

Don's care about time extended to the interviews themselves. Usually I allow the length of an interview to be set by the tape recorder. When the cassette clicks off we stop; occasionally, when the discussion is in the middle of something that cannot wait, I put in a new tape. No one except Don ever stopped in the middle of a tape; he did so almost every time. (I should add that within those time limits he was unusually open.)

At first, Don's description of what he called "stress" seemed unrelated to his dealings with other people; it did not even seem to have much personal meaning. Not enough sleep, too few hours in the day, and then just at the wrong moment the dishwasher in the halfway house starts leaking into the basement—that is what stress is all about. His description emphasized the somatic experience. Describing a meeting earlier in the day, he said:

> How active I am in the meeting depends not just on my role, but how I feel that day. Today was about average. I was pretty up today. I had a good night's sleep, I was sharp mentally as well as not emotionally down or physically tired. . . . I try to pace myself through a meeting like that so I don't wear myself out, so I have something left of life and energy to go home with. In this sort of work if you don't have a sense of your pace and energy you can burn yourself out and have a hard time finishing the day.

It soon became clear that Don's concern is not limited to his own private agitation. Stress makes him irritable. His first reaction, he says, is "anger. Frustrated anger. Oh, why this?" At work, his frustration with the pressure may lead him to bark at his staff: "At Greenpeace House it is an impossible time frame. I set myself schedules, speed up, drive myself: 'It's-got-to-be-done-this-week.' So I will be more directive, more curt, pushing, expecting that people will know what has to be done and losing my sense of proportion of where they are."

I have no evidence that Don's threshold for frustration is in fact lower than anyone else's; what is striking is the unusual care he takes not to become irritated. After a meeting or at the end of the day, he explains, "I always make a clear separation out, so that I am not still processing it. . . . I try to leave it so when I walk in the door I am ready to deal with the dog, my wife and the kids, and not force them to deal with me. That is a high priority for me, one of my highest value statements. When I go home I am available, not demanding. . . . I try not to be a burden, as much as humanly possible."

Two ideas in this passage are critical: Don's concern that his own aggravation will become a burden to someone else, and his technique for managing himself, captured in the phrase, "separating out." What is most important, Don says, is that you do not become "part of the problem." Here he describes the difficulty he faces as a psychotherapist:

> To the degree that you overidentify with the client's definition of the problem you lose the bubble. You know how in power plants they have those bubbling power gauges? The bubble goes out of range when the pressure goes up, or it drops . . . it really goes out of sight. Clinically, when I lose the bubble I have lost my sense of not just objectivity but perception of where I am, where the client is, the whole transference-countertransference dynamic. . . . Where you really lose the bubble is where you become part of the problem; the countertransference gets out of whack and you get hooked into it. That can be innocuous . . . or as radical as engaging in sexual activity with the client. . . . But anyway, that is a little digression; I have forgotten where we started.

Of course, Don is absolutely correct about the danger of becoming emotionally entangled in his clients' lives; still, his concern seems unusually keen. In a different interview he remembered having much the same concern about his obligations in the Navy. "I had to know certain things about how the ship was set up so that if there was an emergency, you couldn't be a liability." His fear—on board ship, as a therapist or as an administrator—seems to be that in a moment of crisis he will somehow lose control, become entangled in the problem, and end up making everything worse. We do not know yet what lies behind this fear. We can see that against this danger, Don adopts a style of emotional distance, "separating out."

One version of this coping style is for Don to keep separate his work life and home. He says, "I shift roles: theological, Naval, mental health, and personal roles. I consciously move from one to another, and behave differently in each." The way Don puts this suggests an image of himself as technically appropriate, but perhaps never unreservedly expressive. Viewed in this way, life becomes a series of tasks, each requiring a clear head, unencumbered by the leftovers of the hour before.

Don is not unemotional; certainly no one would describe him as cold. Yet when he says that his highest value is to be available he seems to wish he were an instrument of service, purified of any personal neediness. Something of this is captured in two very different descriptions:

> If I can't, as a husband and father, be available to my family in the limited time I have, then I am cheating them. The primary responsibility is to shift roles, to be available to the client, to [my boss], to my wife. I try to be a helpful person. . . . Lately one of my highest priorities is to help [the children] with their homework. I am good at algebra and literature, my wife at grammar. Between us we have a lot of the skills; we can transfer that to the kids.

Everyone—the client, the boss, the wife and kids—gets the same thing from Don. They all get his undivided attention. Fatherhood becomes the transfer of skills, an oddly technical description, shorn of emotion. I must emphasize that Don clearly loves his children very much, enjoys being with them, and is probably a very good father. What his language reveals is a particular anxiety: what must he do not to become part of the problem? Here is the same idea in a different form: "[In the Navy] if anyone was getting in trouble [the officers] would automatically use the chaplain. They would use you as a functioning part of the organization. [In one case] someone was considered a security risk. They thought he might not do his job; it was an ideological block. If he doesn't, the machine doesn't work—the ship." Once again, man as instrument is the theme. The ship's officers "use" Don as a functioning part; the sailor whose political beliefs were dangerously strong might not function as part of the machine that is the ship.

Don's concern about becoming "part of the problem" is the first of two principal themes that run through his life. The second is his suspicion that he is not being taken seriously, or that he is being excluded. He remarked, "In the parish, clergy are put on a pedestal of sorts, but at the same time considered somewhat irrelevant to the real world. It is a crazy thing. You are given a high status, yet you are not of this world. I was always uncomfortable with that. I liked parish work, but I didn't like that split. Part of my thought as person is to be more in things, not separate from things."

It was because Don felt patronized and excluded from the company of working men that he chose to serve his ministry outside the traditional parish setting. Don does not consider his current vocation a departure from religious service. Instead, he views his chaplaincy, and now his work as a counseling psychologist, as a way of serving God while being more engaged with this world. In the Navy, Don was a chaplain but also an officer. He is distinctly proud of his acceptance by the other military men: "In the service I really was a Naval officer who happened to be a chaplain also. I participated in the normal functions of the ship. I caught a sense of the difference. . . . What I discovered was to really participate in the life of the people you deal with, there is a different sort of thing going on. It feels better. A lot of avenues of communication opened, and credibility."

The principal occupations in which Don has found himself—minister and psychologist—are each notable for the distance they require between practitioner and clients. From this perspective, Don's career history appears a continual movement toward fuller engagement. Being a chaplain is more worldly than being a parish minister; a counselor is still more worldly; psychological administration does not require even the therapist's detachment. Yet if Don's current occupation no longer sets him apart from his fellows, it is apparent that even in his work as an administrator he feels a distance between himself and his colleagues. Here he describes a meeting with Sam and Jack, his superiors in the organization, that took place on the morning of our second interview:

> Most of the time I was not the most verbally dominant person in the group. . . . [Partly] this relates to who was at the meeting, the fact that they are all long-standing relationships. It is easier for me to be childlike with people I am more comfortable with. . . . This meeting was probably the most important I have had for two months. When I am involved in all that heavy stuff, part of me needs comic relief. . . . Jack and Sam were going at each other in their inimitable way. I was more reacting, laughing uproariously, almost falling off my chair. People say I have always had an infectious laugh. [Sam and Jack] are coequals in the power structure; their repartee calls the shots. . . . Obviously it was humorous, jibing stuff between two equals, males, that sets up certain stuff. Several sexist comments were made. . . . That humor is acceptable if you know the group, not if you don't.

Don begins by saying that this was a meeting with people he has known for a long time, and with whom he feels perfectly comfortable. But as he goes along we begin to wonder. Although he describes laughing uproariously, it is easy to hear in this the nervous laughter of a youngster not quite comfortable with the competitive thrust and parry of the bigger boys. Don emphasizes that he was included: "We are just a bunch of boys, joking about the girls." What he does not say in so many words is that he is included in ways that make him not the equal of the others: he has an infectious sense of humor, he is childlike. We are left wondering how included he really feels. This meeting sounds like the Sam and Jack Show. Don seems aware, even if he does not quite say so, that he was trying too hard to join in, and not quite succeeding.

These two themes—Don's concern about becoming part of the problem, and his sense of exclusion—reappear time and again in his account. In a moment I will describe how these same themes appear in Don's childhood history, and what I suspect are still their unconscious meaning. But first it bears repeating how ordinary, how innocuous, these first descriptions are. Don does not start out telling us that he fears becoming part of the problem; he is worried about getting enough sleep and organizing his schedule. Only a pursuit of suggestive phrases—a pursuit that Don himself would never entertain—has led us to notice Don's dilemma: he wants to be included, but fears becoming destructively enmeshed. Don himself notices nothing of the sort. He explains himself, and relies on our shared understanding, in terms of the sort of interpersonal relationships that are appropriate in the work world. I will return to this point, and its relation to unconscious meaning, after we understand Don's history.

History

Don was born with a twin brother. During birth, the umbilical cord became twisted around the brother's neck so that oxygen was cut off. The brother died twelve days later.

What did this death mean to Don? Did he think about it much when he was a child? Did he hold himself responsible? Don himself recalls very little aside from his childhood thought that it would have been fun to have a playmate. But certain other pieces of information and images that have stayed with Don since childhood suggest the line his thinking may have taken.

Occasionally I ask the people I interview about their earliest memories. (Psychoanalytic theory suggests that these memories reveal, in highly symbolic images, prevailing life themes.) One of Don's earliest memories is of watching his father fix the incubator for the chickens. Why should this odd image have escaped the usual amnesia of childhood? Later, Don mentioned that his brother was put in a shoebox in the oven. The oven served as an incubator. By itself, the image is elusive. All it suggests is that the brother's brief life and death were a preoccupation for Don, preserved now in the elliptical image of the incubator that might have saved his life, but did not.

Don knows that his parents were not expecting twins. His brother received the one name picked in advance—he was named after the father—while Don himself was named after the doctor. The history of the names could add to a child's thought, "He was the real baby; I wasn't supposed to be there, and that is what killed him." Of course we are speculating here on what might be true, based on very little that Don has said directly. But what Don tells us of this early death—an account that he knew as a child—connects to other themes that we have heard repeatedly in his adult life. Don feels that he was not expected, not "included" by his family, and that by his unexpected, intrusive appearance he became "part of the problem" that killed his brother.

Don's father died of a heart attack when Don was seven.

We had just gotten through with the tug-of-war at the picnic. My father's side had won, and we were all excited. I remember being on the bench, hanging on to him, trying to get on his shoulders or something, and he was saying, "I'm tired, just bug off." Something to that effect. And as it turned out he was having a heart attack. And then he got up and collapsed a

few feet away. A lot of people came around and I was excluded.... They put him in an
ambulance and we followed the ambulance, being helpless and cut off, the adults taking
over, that whole sense of being detached.

Here the implication that Don caused a death is more clearly stated. Here too,
he remembers feeling excluded. The adults take over, the child goes
unnoticed.

The shock waves of the father's death led to even more disruption. The
family moved to Kalamazoo, where Don's mother had family. A half-sister,
the father's daughter by a previous marriage, went off to live with her
grandparents. Don himself made a few friends in town, but since his school
was far from the neighborhood where they lived he was once again isolated.
Worse, he felt somewhat excluded within his family. His mother and older
sister drew closer while he turned inward. For a time he became chubby. (He is
now definitely on the thin side.) Relief came from the families of his friends
and relatives across town.

I was fortunate to have a lot of people in the family and outside who would just naturally be
supportive of me as a person. Relatives always thought of me as a nice guy; they liked
having me around.... People in the church always treated me with a lot of respect.... As a
kid, I wasn't just looked down on. Some of the fathers of other kids would include you, take
you fishing. You'd feel included. "Gee, Don, I'm really glad you could come."

Here I asked, "What was it they liked about you?" He replied,

As an adult and as a kid, I'm a "nice guy." I'm not mean. I heard someone say in college that
a gentleman is someone who never intentionally hurts another person. That struck me. That
sort of captures me in a way. I will certainly unintentionally hurt people; we all do. But I
always consciously try to be a positive influence, not something that drags things down or is
negative.

One more time the twin themes of being a nice kid who would never hurt
anyone, and being treated with respect and included, come together. By now
we have enough to sketch the outlines of an interpretation.

The dilemma that poses itself everywhere in Don's life can be put as a
question: "How can I be included without becoming destructive?" The terms
of this dilemma refer back to many different moments in his history: his sense
of isolation within his own family after his father's death, his belief that he was
welcomed by other children's parents because he was "a nice kid," his fear that
he caused his father's heart attack by clinging to him, his memory of feeling
excluded by the adults who "took over" on the way to the hospital, and his
childhood suspicion that he was not included in his parents' expectations and
that his intrusive presence killed his brother.

Piecing the story together now, the historical order of events may appear to be a causal order as well. That is, we are tempted to say that Don's earliest understanding of his brother's death (and the part Don imagined he played in it) colored his interpretation of the father's heart attack. In turn, both events influenced Don's experience of his later isolation within his own family and his acceptance by others. But although something like this must have happened, the order of influence would not have been nearly as one-directional as this chronology suggests. At various points along the way, Don must have reinterpreted earlier events in the light of later experience. In fact, he might remember the past differently as new experiences changed his conception of the world.

This reciprocal influence of the past and present upon each other means that we can never say of any event, "This is really where it all began." The brother's death is not the fundamental tragedy in Don's life to which all subsequent experience refers, nor is the father's heart attack. But both of these deaths, continually reinterpreted in the light of later experience, do remain very much alive in Don's current concern that on ship, in his office or at home he might intrude, and so become "part of the problem."

How much of this could Don acknowledge? Probably not very much at all in any but the most intellectualized sense. Our interpretation of his guiltiness and isolation, and his attempt to correct both by being dispassionately available, must rest on more than he could say directly. Still, here is a passage that comes close.

> D: Christ speaks of being the leaven. . . . In order for evil to succeed, good men must do nothing. Being like yeast is a calculated sort of thing, not just passively nice. Without making a bad thing worse, you work to make a bad thing better.
>
> RO: Without making a bad thing worse? . . . You seem to be always aware of that possibility.
>
> D: Oh yes, that was clearly in focus when I was in the service.
>
> RO: How about as a kid?
>
> D: Oh yeah, though I can't recall anything.
>
> RO: What about your father dying, or your brother?
>
> D: I don't recall any strong feelings about that.

I am sure he doesn't, but that does not change a thing. If my interpretation is right, then the meaning of stress and its connection to not being part of the problem becomes intelligible. Don has devoted himself to a life of dispassionate service. The antecedents of this style (and, I must emphasize, its current unconscious meaning) can be traced to both the wish to be included and respected, and the hope that he is not the cause of trouble. For "trouble" we may read, at its most frightening extreme, death.

Don is reluctant to think about these matters, he has found a ready defense in the culture of work. The vocations Don has pursued—the ministry, psychotherapy and, with some stylistic differences, administration—all encourage work relationships that strike a balance between personal engagement and detachment. This balance should not be underestimated. Work culture certainly does not prescribe an impersonal, machinelike world. In this study, the personal politics of business is a theme touched on by almost every subject. At the same time, work culture insists on a boundary between appropriate collegiality and the intrusion of one's personal concerns.

Don describes himself in terms that capture this balance nicely. He has a lively sense of humor; he specifically mentions the importance of personal warmth in therapy. Yet his description of his humor and warmth renders even these personal qualities as technical skills. In his description of the meeting, laughter is a strategy he employs to cut the tension. The personal touch is necessary to therapeutic success.

In later cases, Ken and Bob will describe the tactical advantage to which business puts the personal touch. For Don, calling it a tactical consideration seems to get the point exactly backwards. Don is not trying to gain an advantage by being personal; he is trying to be helpful. In another sense, the term may not be so out of place after all. Don is in the business of being helpful, and not only as a therapist. Being personal is part of his professional style. This is true whether we are speaking of him as therapist, as minister, or in his "role" of family man. Since Don has made a career of helpfulness, his version of personalism is not aimed at securing an advantage. Yet his, too, is a style of applied friendliness. In his own way, his version of professional personalism is not so different from men in more competitive occupations.

The alliance of culture and psyche seems to work to everyone's benefit. Don gets a reprieve from thinking about things that would, at least initially, be disturbing. His employers get an effective performer. But on closer examination, the benefits seem less equally distributed.

The bargain Don has struck requires him to pay certain costs. His coping strategy of "separating out" is intended to assure him that the agitation of work will not invade his home, and that his private cares will not interfere with his performance on the job. But the bulwark thus erected proves leaky. Don's concern about his job seems to invade his home life to a considerable degree. Sitting in his living room, talking to me, he remarked that the phone might ring at any moment with an emergency. In his effort to contain work, he actually begins two hours before breakfast. Once he is at work, he remains preoccupied by the thought that "stress" may damage his efficiency; much of his time is devoted to anti-stress maneuvering.

On the other side of the coin, being "available" and "nice" promises Don that he can be engaged with people in ways that felt closed to him as a child. But here too his success seems limited. I have called attention to the peculiarly detached tone of his service-machine style. At home, "being available" allows Don to offer himself to his children and his wife. It is less clear whether Don can permit others to know him. His version of engagement is one-sided and, we might suspect, ultimately lonely.

"Niceness" suffers a different limitation. As a child, Don lost an extraordinary number of important people. He learned that being nice was one way to be included in other children's family outings. As an adult, however, being nice no longer really corrects the emotional detachment Don feels. The reason has to do with a different meaning of niceness and detachment.

Don's history and his own words strongly suggest that he fears his capability for doing damage. Being a "nice guy" demonstrates that he is not reprehensible, he is not the sort of person who would ever hurt anyone knowingly. But Don's preoccupation with never hurting others prevents him from being aggressive when it would be appropriate. For this reason, Don continues to sound like a child in the company of adults. In his own words, he is still being "childlike," the nice boy with an infectious sense of humor, at business meetings. No wonder he feels that others never quite take him seriously. Ultimately, "niceness" undermines what he really wants: to be included as a man among men.

The symmetry between Don's own ambivalence—his wish to be engaged yet dispassionate—and the similarly two-sided expectation in the culture of work might tempt us to imagine that Don has found a solution, a vocational niche that mirrors his psychological needs. But this is not quite accurate. Don has a problem: some of the things he wants are opposed to others. He wants to be taken seriously but he also wants to be a nice guy. He wants to be effective but he does not want to become a problem to anyone. He may be able to have it all, at different times, but that would require him to feel sure of himself in ways that the self-image of acting in role undermines.

The idea of acting in role promises him a solution. He can shift roles and so be appropriate everywhere. But the promise falls short. It takes up an evaluative position outside of Don, one that judges emotion by its utility. In agreeing to look at the matter this way, Don becomes a mystery to himself. He abdicates subjective self-knowledge and self-control. It is unlikely that he would see the problem in these terms. These are terms that deliberately attempt to resubjectivize an experience that he has chosen to look at—a choice abetted by his culture—from the perspective of those who make use of him. Don would not think his problem is that of self-knowledge; he thinks it is stress. It is only we who realize the two are the same.

4

Nothing Personal

Ken Evans describes himself as the chief operations officer of a tool and die company. An operations officer, he explains, is the executive who deals with people instead of numbers. "I'm analogous to a coach," he says.

The business was started forty years ago by Ken's father and two partners. Eighteen years ago Ken's older brother, Jack, joined the company and for six years Jack, the father, and the two other partners ran the business. In 1970, at the invitation of the brother and against the preference of the father, Ken also joined. The father retired two stormy years later. The brothers bought out the other partners and a good chunk of the father's stock as well. Today they run the company together.

In title, Jack, who is older by seven years, is president. In practice Ken runs the show. Under his driving leadership the company's business grew from $2 million a year to $8 million within a three-year span. Now, while most others in Michigan's shell-shocked auto industry are in retreat, the company is gearing up for another major expansion.

Personally, Ken is the incarnation of aggressive, ambitious success. Years ago he was an All-American gymnast at Indiana University. Now at thirty-seven the muscle looks a shade rounder and the glasses tone down his physical presence. Yet he still speaks loudly and quickly, bearing down on a conversation until he owns it.

By good fortune my interviews caught Ken during the heart of a critical transition in the business. At Ken's initiative the brothers hired a business consultant. Ostensibly the consultant was brought in to advise them on their plans for expansion. Actually the consultant was Ken's idea of how to break a conflict that has been building between him and Jack. For about three years, Jack has been paying less attention to the business. He arrives late and leaves early. Worse, as Ken sees it, Jack ignores critical decisions that only the company president should make. Eventually, and always with time running out, these decisions fall to Ken. He has been company president in all but name for several years. Ken says he wants Jack to pull his weight, to either act like a president or turn the job over to him. The consultant agrees. Under his guidance the brothers are now negotiating a shift in jobs. Ken will become president, Jack chairman of the board.

The consultation itself includes a detailed psychological profile of every employee. These profiles are potentially open to inspection by anyone in the company. There is a standard format, suggested by the consultant, whereby any two employees can disclose their profiles to each other. Ken looks forward to this inaugurating a new era of mutual understanding and team effort.

Two changes have resulted from the consultation. The most dramatic, of course, is Ken's elevation to the presidency. But a second issue preoccupied Ken through our interviews, and will serve as the focus of our attention. In his investigation the consultant discovered that one employee is cordially detested by almost everyone in the company. Ken has been aware of this man's abrasive personality for some time, yet firing him would be difficult. He is one of the oldest employees, a student Ken brought with him to the plant from his brief stint as a teacher. Ken has taken Mike on as a protégé, and, what is perhaps harder to admit, a friend. Among other considerations, Ken saw Mike through a divorce a few years ago. Now, Ken discovers, his employees are beginning to grumble. One even told the consultant, "Mike must be blackmailing Ken for him to put up with this."

Ken has been outraged by Mike's behavior. As Ken sees it, Mike has not only betrayed a friendship, he has exploited Ken's affection, turned it to his own advantage, and left Ken feeling exposed and humiliated: "The feeling is extreme disappointment on my part. He doesn't either respect me, or care enough about me to do his job.... Instead of saying, 'Ken, I will do twice as good this time, for you, because you are giving me this chance,' he takes it as a sign of weakness: 'That means I can can screw off even more.'" There seems little doubt that Mike is in fact performing poorly. Firing him would certainly be reasonable, though perhaps not the only choice. Yet in the course of our interviews it became clear that Ken is unusually troubled by this case. The options he sees and the logic with which he understands them are the focus of this study.

After much consideration, Ken decided not to fire Mike, but to strip him of all managerial responsibility and offer him instead a straight sales job, with a base salary half what Mike had been earning and a possibility of making up some of the difference in commissions. Ken said he knew very well it was a harsh offer, one that Mike might not be able to live with. At that point I asked, "If you have decided not to fire Mike, why not cut his salary to some more livable figure in between?" Ken replied, "I could do that, but that kind of prostitutes the whole thing.... If I cut him by twenty-five percent it is like bleeding him to death. You know this way I am severing an arm, or two arms, and then throwing him out there. But at least I am giving him a viable choice."

When we returned to this question in the next interview, Ken offered a somewhat different rationale: "Well, let's say he could live with $25,000 a year, is he going to be an effective salesman? I don't know. In that case I'll end up having to fire him [anyway], or I am stuck with an ineffective salesman, and he is bitter at that point. . . . He can walk away or say, 'I don't like it, but I think I can do it, and I am going to give it a shot.' " In this passage Ken suggests the first of several themes that are condensed in his decision about Mike, but that also recur throughout his life story: the danger of unexpressed, festering rancor and the virtue of bold surgery. Speaking of a different business dispute that he nipped in the bud, Ken said, "If you don't squelch it right away it will fester; go down the ladder [of the company organization], and all of a sudden you have a real serious problem."

In the same vein, Ken is determined to get all of his grievances with Jack out on paper, in a formal agreement of expectations. Ken says he is afraid that anything he does not say now he will have to live with later. If for some reason the new arrangement does not work out, Ken is determined to force a denouement:

> I am not prepared to put up with it again. I would force the issue next time. Just continue antagonizing the issue until a decision would have to be made. . . . I would rather fight it as hard as I can, with everything I have, than sit back and say, "This is how it will be forever more." That would tear me up. . . . It would bother me less to lose my brother's friendship as a result of going on the attack to straighten up the situation.

Finally, there is one remarkable passage in which Ken speculates on the possible reasons that his brother lost interest in the business: "I have talked with him, but I can't get him out of his shell. I hear about his wife and kids, but I don't hear the real issue. . . . It has got to be more than what he is experiencing at home, because that is something you can correct. You can always get a divorce, walk away from it, chalk it up to experience and go on to the next thing. You don't destroy your life for that kind of aggravation." At first, Ken considers the possibility that his brother may be having trouble at home. But then he concludes, "No, this cannot be the reason. You can always sever a marriage." From a different angle this repeats the idea that no one should put up with a festering sore. You have to cut off the rotten limb and walk away from it.

Ken offered a second explanation of why it was important to punish Mike harshly and publicly: this is a moment of transition for the company. Ken is taking over as president and he wants to lead the company sharply away from what he sees as his brother's mismanagement. He wants his employees to know that a decisive leader is now at the helm. He also wants to encourage a style of collegiality among his middle management. Toward this end, he hopes that his staff will share their psychological profiles with each other as a way of building mutual understanding. These managerial considerations also play into his decision about Mike:

People expect this situation to be resolved in a legitimate manner.... We are going through an awful lot of changes right now, with people exposing themselves.... it is a new feeling. Plus, Jack was a waffling type president; I'd like to change that. This guy happens to be part of that image. It isn't strictly personal; there is a much bigger picture in here.... You know, if they are going to expose themselves, and try to make a contribution, the company is going to have to make some sort of contribution too, and do it in a forthright, honest manner.

Up to a point, Ken's explanation is plausible. The employees do resent Ken's seeming partiality, and probably want him to deal with the situation decisively. But Ken goes a step further in suggesting that punishing Mike will reassure everyone about the consultant's behavioral analysis, and make it easier for them to share their profiles with each other. This seems less likely. After all, Mike got in trouble because of what the consultant discovered. The other employees may now be saying, "This consultant is a dangerous guy. He finds out things about you, and then you lose your job. If even a favorite like Mike isn't immune, why on earth should I risk that kind of exposure?" For some reason, Ken never considers this possibility.

Like the danger of festering anger, the risk and virtue of self-exposure is a constant theme in Ken's story. Ken has a vivid sense of the potential for humiliation in disclosure. Several times he said, "The behavior analysis is like having your pants pulled down in the middle of a football field." He imagines showing the consultant's report to his father, and the embarrassment that would cause Jack. For all his talk of clean, open anger, he is keenly aware that Mike's reaction to his demotion will likely be unforgivable shame. Ken has even attempted to capitalize on the potential for embarrassment. In the new organization, each brother will appoint a personal friend to the Board. Ken firmly anticipates that this will force Jack to take a more active role. After all, Jack would be ashamed to have a personal friend see him as incompetent.

The risk and attraction in self-disclosure is not limited to business; the same theme figures in prominently in Ken's discussion of friendship:

I don't like insensitive people. I want people as friends who aren't afraid of talking about all kinds of different issues.... I like people that expose enough of themselves that they are vulnerable; that's a real friend as far as I am concerned.... It has to be totally open but totally trusting too. If it is one thing that destroys a friendship it is where you say something in confidence and all of a sudden it comes back to you from someone else. That only happens once; that is almost intolerable. The wall is there from then on.

Closely related to the idea of exposure and shame is Ken's fear of being provoked into saying more than he intended, and so losing power. As Ken sees it, a large part of business strategy is an attempt to seduce an opponent—or provoke him—into revealing something that can be exploited. He describes how he and his management team will rehearse for a meeting with union representatives, so as not to be thrown by them:

The union reps work like a classical debate guy. They will antagonize you intentionally to get you or your subordinates to say something that they can pick up on.... So I will [tell my subordinates], "If something is brought up on this particular thing just ignore it and stay away from it." People may not know they are being controlled, but I am controlling that meeting. I can have a surrogate in there talking on a certain issue, but it has been role-played beforehand and I am in total control of that situation.

In this example the danger of saying too much at first sounds impersonal. An injudicious comment might give away a bargaining position. But a close reading of the passage suggests a more personal concern. Ken fears that the union representative might provoke his anger. If he did, Ken might say too much, he might expose himself, and so lose power. Provocation leads to exposure and defeat. Here it is again:

I deal with a lot of machinery salesmen, and they are really aggressive guys. It is a rough business, real competitive; steel and machinery are like that. And they are professionals at dominating a sales meeting: "sign up, sign up, do this, do that." So what I like to do is encroach on their so-called perimeter, really cut their defenses down. So what I end up doing is this. [Here he moved his chair very close to mine and leaned forward.] I play the body language thing, get really close, until the guy is uneasy, the sweat is pouring out of him, he doesn't know what the hell is going on. Pretty soon he is totally out of control, he is so anxious to get out of there.... And I found that once you pull that type of thing all of a sudden your relationship changes. Next time it will be more as if I were a peer and not some guy where they have to put the move on him.

Ken's description of what he calls "body language"—moving his chair in close—is interesting. It presents, in physical images, the kind of emotional manipulation he described a moment before. The union representatives, he said, gain their advantage by provoking. In a telling phrase that he might have used, they "get under your skin." They get too close. In this description, Ken turns getting too close to his advantage. The question of distance and emotional control is an idea that will return.

The most telling line in the passage may be the last: "I'm not some guy where they have to put the move on him." The phrase, with its connotations of cynical, degrading seduction, captures Ken's fear. Something of the same thought emerges in a very different passage. When Ken meets with buyers he takes them to a football game, or fishing, rather than to play golf. "I hate the goddamn game. Why should I put myself into such frustration chasing some stupid white ball around because some guy I am selling to happens to enjoy that kind of masochistic game?" The danger in revealing yourself is more than giving away information; you leave yourself open to being demeaned. The union rep can make you angry, the buyer may humiliate you. Even the "masochism" of golf fits here: the danger is of abasement.

At some point, after hearing this refrain enough times to recognize it, I began to wonder why a man so acutely sensitive to exposure would agree to these interviews. Ken's answer was revealing:

> I don't have any problem with it. It depends how it is being used. You are using it as a professional person, trying to *get* something out of it. If we sat down at a bar stool and you started pumping me for information I'd probably walk away, not say a word. But in this structure it is just like the behavioral analysis. It is the setting, discussing it with your employees where there is some mutual gain, [as opposed to] discussing it with a friend where they don't understand you in a business situation.

Ken's comparison of these interviews to the behavioral analysis makes the point. This is business. Interestingly enough, the critical idea may be "You are getting something out of this." Under the aegis of self-interest and the impersonality it guarantees, Ken is willing to discuss aspects of his life that he would guard from all but his closest friends.

As he sees it, the same logic explains why his employees should cooperate with the consultant. Of course Ken is not naive. He acknowledges that cooperation, nominally optional, is less than voluntary for his hired workers. Yet even so he assumes that the behavioral analysis appears legitimate to his employees. After all, it is not "really" asking about their personal lives; only their business personalities are in question.

This brings us, by way of a large circle, to the point where we began. Ken is actually committed to the idea of self-exposure, as long as it is limited to business. He draws a subtle—but for him, critical—distinction between the kind of self-revelation that fosters collegiality and the kind that risks losing power.

Ken began, as I mentioned, by describing himself as the people person in his company, the "coach," in contrast to his brother, whom Ken pictures as a cold statistician. Jack conducts his work behind the closed door of his office. He does not know or care about the men who work for him. A small company cannot be run this way, Ken declares. You need the personal loyalty of your employees. Ken actively courts this loyalty with dinners, invitations to his home, and an interest in his employees' families. "You have to take a key employee to dinner with his wife, to find out whether she supports his endeavors and to try to engender support in her. Because if you don't have both people you will never be effective. You don't want her complaining [when he has to work late]. You have to sit down with his wife and explain your feelings about her husband, how important he is, and how much you rely on him."

Ken contrasts his managerial style not only with Jack's but with their father's. As Ken sees it, his father is obsessed with a fear of exposing any chink of vulnerability. Bringing your employee to your house is an invitation to resentment, especially if the house is as luxurious as Ken's. Ken describes this guardedness as only the father's misanthropy. Yet, as we have heard, the suspicion he sees in his father is also a refrain in his own philosophy. Don't expose anything to anyone except proven friends, or they will have power over you.

Although Ken prides himself on his ability to establish personal relationships with his staff, he draws a careful distinction between the sociability of business colleagues and genuine friendship. The invitations to dinner or to his house are strictly in the interests of promoting business harmony. There is no question of real trust developing.

> I am not saying that people who work for me, that it is a standoffish kind of relationship. We get into good discussions and understand each other, and talk very frankly about certain issues, but there is still a natural barrier that inhibits it from going from the sixty-fifth percentile to the ninety-eighth—whatever. It just can't be; it has to be guarded. It can't [become a friendship] because I am in a control position. I have got too much influence on their normal sphere of life, and that kind of relationship doesn't work.

There is a problem with becoming too chummy with your subordinates, Ken observes: it becomes that much harder to discipline them.

> If someone is not doing a good job it is your obligation to terminate him. It is twice as hard if you are close. You are better off being aloof if you are going to be a terminator. . . . I have never fired anyone who didn't deserve it, and hadn't received direct warning, and been told about their severance. "When you leave, you will leave that minute. Pack up your stuff and be gone." I have never terminated someone who hasn't come back to see me. I spent an hour on the phone with someone at Christmas. He said it was the best thing that ever happened to him. And he learned more from me than anyone else.

More than coincidentally, the man whom Ken is describing here was fired for getting himself into exactly the bind Ken is warning against. The man became too close to a subaltern and was unable to discipline him effectively. "He was not an effective supervisor. He could not separate the ability to relate to people and the ability to discipline them at the same time. I told him, 'Today is the day,' and we shook hands."

Officially at least, firing is an impersonal business. There is no call for hard feelings. Of course, Ken's insistence that the employee clear out his desk and leave immediately is an odd note. It suggests what we have begun to suspect: that for Ken, the boundary between personal ties and bottom line impersonality is shaky, and can only be maintained by extremism. We will return to this in a moment.

The first interview closed with Ken musing on the mutual understanding of a boss and his employees:

A manager has to understand his people, but also be honest. When you relate with them in a social situation it is not a true social situation. It is a mutual thing. They are getting something out of it and so am I. It isn't indeed a true, honest friendship because I have too much control. I sign the check. I would never trust them as a friend because I don't know if am getting true feelings back or brownnosing. And they wouldn't trust me, because they are thinking, "What does he want now?" When I have them in it is more so they can know me better and vice versa. But certain people can't separate that; they get hooked in. They are nice people, but I have a role to play. Put bread on the table for all my people. If I don't, I am jeopardizing everyone. That is my role.

Although Ken does not mention Mike by name, these passages explain his position toward Mike. Ken's decision to discipline him is impersonal, it is what his employees expect, it is the only way a business can be run. All of this may be true. By now, however, we have heard too much to believe that this is the entire story. In ways that are not yet clear, Ken feels that Mike has demeaned him. Ken worries about festering anger—whose anger is unclear— and about his employees' confidence in self-disclosure. Disciplining Mike is supposed to repair these injuries. But here, Ken's logic, cast as simply a business decision, is less pursuasive. And so we must look elsewhere for its meaning, not in the official explanation of business practice, but in more private and uncomfortable reasons.

History

At first, the story Ken told of his childhood seemed to offer little insight. Most of my questions were deflected with clichés: a wonderful father with "a brilliant mind" who took him fishing and hunting every weekend, a fine mother, a sunny, active childhood as the apparently favored son. But as we continued to talk Ken began to tell a different story. Gradually, it became clear that his relationship with his father had been difficult for a very long time.

At one point Ken mentioned how much his father detests Ken's sociable managerial style. "If he were dead," Ken said, "he would turn over in his grave." What is his father like? The picture Ken presented is mixed. His father is often uncomfortable socially, perhaps because he is uneducated and afraid of saying something embarrassing. He is not always shy. He can be witty and charming at parties once his wife breaks the ice. But his stories are all about himself. Ken feels that he is totally uninterested in other people. The few times that Ken has approached his father with a problem he has been rebuffed. For instance, last year Ken tried to ask his father about Jack. Was there some trouble at home that might explain his brother's attitude at work?

I ended up getting a two hour tirade. That it was none of my business, and I shouldn't be interfering. It ended up that my father's pension wasn't big enough, and both me and my brother had screwed him royally. I ended up just raked over the coals for problems I never knew existed. "Here you are concerned about your brother and you are not even concerned about your own Dad."

The father has always had a violent and unpredictable temper. Ken sees these outbursts as indirect and manipulative. Somehow they never clear the air.

His method of disciplining [an employee] was to stand near him, call him every bad thing in the book but not face to face, so the guy is ready to kill you. But never say anything direct. . . .

He controls situations by being inconsistent. His emotions are inconsistent. . . . He has to be right, and how he approaches being right could be anything from calling you a son of a bitch to overwhelming you with affection.

At home:

My Dad handles [arguments] the same as at work. He yells, blows up, calls you every name in the book, then ten minutes later gives you a hug and says, "Why are you so upset?" [Laughs.] You are ready to kill him at that point, and he can't understand it. "What's the matter, got a chip on your shoulder?" After he has totally abused you. . . .

He will say anything. He is just vicious when he goes on the attack. . . . [An hour later] he'd say that I am carrying a grudge, you know without any apology or discussion. It was just expected to be dropped. He has vented his feelings and that is all there is to it; he is done with it.

When Ken was a child most of the father's anger was vented at Jack, who was then a wild, irresponsible teenager. Ken avoided most of his father's temper, partly by playing the exemplary child.

K: You watch it, the yelling and screaming and flipping off the deep end, and then cooling off. It was something I didn't want to mess with. I just didn't do things that were wrong; I was a more exemplary child.

RO: What did you do?

K: Well, in my middle years, the gymnastics. And I was an Eagle Scout.

At this point we must read between the lines, filling in more than Ken has said directly. Perhaps he did escape most of his father's wrath. Yet the vividness with which he describes those tirades suggests that they left their impression. Perhaps a different child could have played by the same volatile rules, shrugging off the thunder. For whatever reason, Ken could not. He was left holding the bag: steaming, inarticulate, and chided for holding a grudge. Small wonder that he still sees anger as a shady device in a manipulative game, or that he feels so keenly the danger of unexpressed resentment.

The next image is of Ken at seventeen. He won a gymnastics scholarship to Indiana, enrolled in engineering, and discovered that one or the other will have to go. In his sophomore year he made All-American. At the same time he was on academic probation (gymnastics took six hours' practice a day). At the rate he was going graduation in four years was impossible, but four years was all the scholarship an athlete received. Indiana was not likely to pick up the tab for an athlete who had outlived his eligibility. Ken decided to drop gymnastics in favor of school work, and asked his father for help with tuition. His father refused, saying he could not afford it.

Here I asked for figures. At first Ken upheld his father's view: $3,000 was a lot of money in 1964. Then again his father's income at the time—Ken estimates $27,000—was no small amount either. Still, he is reluctant to dispute his father's decision. Maybe money was not the real issue.

K: I think he thought, you know, "If he drops out of gymnastics he could drop out of school too."

RO: Was that a possibility in your mind too?

K: Yeah, I think it was. I felt kind of defeated; that was the first time in my life. . . . I couldn't succeed academically and continue gymnastics. That is a tough realization; you finally reach your limit. But it was a good lesson. . . . Sports like gymnastics teach you self-discipline, to accept defeats without passing the buck to the other guy.

RO: How did you come to terms with giving it up?

K: Well it wasn't very hard. You knew exactly what it was going to take, and you knew that wasn't what you could do, so it is actually a very pragmatic decision. It was an obvious thing.

There was a solution. Ken switched out of engineering and cut back gymnastics to the bare minimum necessary for his scholarship. This meant giving up hopes for national recognition and turning gymnastics into a half-hearted job. The plan worked; his grades shot up and he graduated on time.

This is another incident in which Ken accepts an "obvious" decision, which may in fact be reasonable, with an explanation that does not actually make sense. Maybe his father could not afford tuition. Maybe he did see a touch of indifference in Ken. Still, it is hard to see how the father's decision can be construed as an attempt to keep Ken from dropping out. It seems to have made staying in school more difficult. To stay in school he needed the scholarship. To keep the scholarship he had to devote time to gymnastics practice, which in turn could have meant not graduating.

What Ken says about this event is like what he says about demoting Mike. Whatever good reasons Ken may have for demoting Mike, it is hard to understand how that decision will reassure anyone about the consultant. In both cases Ken says, "Yes, of course, this was the best decision." But best in what way? Of course, he says, tough self-discipline is better than being bailed out by your father. Of course pragmatic impersonality is better than favoritism. And maybe from a business point of view it is all true. But is it true emotionally?

Recalling the tuition incident now, Ken excuses his father. He claims to see the virtue in not letting your personal affection for someone stop you from being tough. But did he see it that way at eighteen? For that matter, is he telling us the whole truth about how he sees it now?

Ken, who prides himself on his own toughness, rarely acknowledges how deeply he can be hurt. Our evidence has to come indirectly, by juxtaposing comments that he makes in ostensibly unrelated passages. For example, Ken occasionally contrasts his own father with his father-in-law; he sometimes sounds as if he has adopted this man as the father he really wants. The father-in-law is a well-respected man in Grosse Pointe, a man Ken admires for his personal touch. "He really is the one who developed my people orientation, because my family is not people-oriented at all. They are people manipulators, not real sincere. . . . I think that what really impressed me about him is that every time in our married life that we needed something he not only knew about it in advance, he reacted immediately. He just understood people so well."

Here Ken recounted how, when he was first married, the father-in-law provided money for a freezer and "not just financial, but emotional support." The contrast between this unsolicited generosity and the father's tight-fistedness is apparent. The point of course is not just money. The father-in-law listened and cared.

Today, Ken refuses to acknowledge directly what the father-in-law story implies: that he was wounded by his father's stinginess. The business code of impartiality provides Ken with a way to rationalize, retrospectively, a painful event. It turns his relationship with his father, always problematic, into something understandable by the standards of business. Finally, he reenacts the scene with Mike; now he will be sternly impartial. From this angle, firing Mike appears to be more than revenge. It allows Ken to act out, and thereby soldify, the rationalization that protects him from recognizing how pained he was by his father.

Ken graduated from Indiana, then returned to Michigan for a master's degree in business. At that point his father offered him a position in the company, promising a job that would put Ken's business degree to use. Ken demurred, preferring to stay in Lansing and teach at a business school. A year later he decided to take his father up on the offer, but at this point his father said, "There is no job here. If you want to work go into the toolroom." As for a job fit for a business graduate, the father said, "I thought your degree was in art." (Ken had a minor in art history.) Later, in one of his rages, the father swore he had never wanted Ken in the business at all; it had all been Jack's idea. "Maybe he was threatened by me," Ken said. "He knows how aggressive I am. I was going to succeed at something he hadn't accomplished in forty years."

Here Ken noted the irony of Jack's rebelliousness and his own apparent obedience. Jack had been an uncontrollable teenager, but when he came to work for his father he became a docile employee. Ken was the exemplary child—the one who ducked his father's tantrums—but once he got into the firm it was clear he was taking over. Jack only *seemed* to fight back, Ken claims; I was the real threat.

Ken's account of his success in the business underscores a double reversal. He and his brother have switched roles: Jack turns out to be a paper tiger, while Ken's own claws are real. Perhaps more important, Ken says that his father was afraid of him. We can guess what Ken would never say in so many words: Ken was once very afraid of his father. Career success has been Ken's way of defeating a father who tyrannized him as a child.

Throughout Ken's description of himself as an adult he insists upon his credentials as a fighter. Hardly ever does he suggest that as a child he was fearful and ashamed of his reluctance to fight back. But this hypothesis (we cannot be certain) is strongly suggested by the conjunction of what he does remember of his early years and what he passionately insists is not true of himself now. For example, we know that as a child he escaped his father's tirades rather than fight back like his brother. But now, he says, remaining silent in the dispute with his brother "would tear me up. It would bother me less to lose his friendship by going on the attack." In a similar vein, he showed me his own personality profile in the consultant's report, saying that it was eighty percent accurate. The profile, as I read it, sounded diplomatic. It recognized the obvious—Ken's aggressive drive—but suggested that he is willing to listen to another opinion and compromise. I asked, "What was the twenty percent you disagreed with?" fully expecting Ken to explain that he is not really domineering. He replied, "It said that I readily accept other people's opinions; that is not necessarily the case at all.... I won't necessarily subordinate my opinion to another person and compromise—that isn't the way I operate at all! I tend to try to win my position. I will change if I am proven wrong.... I'd rather do that than compromise." These passages, ostensibly about Ken's business career, reveal more about his childhood experience than Ken is willing to admit directly. They suggest how demeaning his childhood intimidation felt.

If the family business is Ken's symbolic battlefield, today he stands on the brink of total victory. Against his father's wishes, he has taken over the company, bought out his partners, driven profits to undreamed-of levels, and soon he will displace his older brother as official president. And yet, even at this moment of triumph, he finds himself the victim of the most astonishingly unjust reversal of all. Somehow his brother, the old hell-raiser and ne'er-do-well, has become his father's favorite. Ken recites a litany of unfair comparisons.

Both brothers received an M.B.A. from The University of Michigan. Ken won the prize as the top student in the program. His parents never came to the award ceremony. "To this day they don't really even acknowledge that I attended Michigan. I mean, they know it, but they don't recognize it as being important. They say, 'Jack went to Michigan, and he has a bachelor's and a master's degree, and Ken went to Indiana.' I don't think they recognize it, or I don't think he does."

Jack is now on the board of a yacht club in Detroit. Ken was on the founding board of a country club in Okemos, a wealthy Lansing suburb. "They didn't know I was on the board! We talked about it, but all the discussion is about Jack."

Recently the brothers invented an industrial gadget. Ken says it was mostly his design, but as far as his parents are concerned it is Jack's device. "Anything worthwhile that both of us do, it's Jack's thing." Then there was the time in Florida:

> We started talking about business, and they were both sitting there patting themselves on the back, on what a wonderful job they had done building the business. I said, "What kind of horse shit is this? Don't you think I have made a viable kind of contribution?" And they said, "Hell no. We could have hired a guy like you; anybody could hire a supervisor. . . . The real contribution was made by Jack and I."
>   . . . At this point I control the whole company. If they don't like it they can both sell their stock. I am in a position to tell them that, and back it up. But at that point I wasn't in any position to do anything other than just take it.

Ken rarely admits, in so many words, how pained he is by his father's rejection. But on the last day we talked—for three hours, this time not sitting in his sunken living room with the big picture window looking out over the lake, or his trophy-lined study, but outside, in his new camper—he admitted for the first time how wounded he had been: "The thing that will always bother me as long as I live is never having had my Dad say that I have done a good job with the business. And he never will say that, I guarantee it, to the day he croaks. And that will always bother me."

The wounds are deep and personal. They have to do with what it means to receive a father's blessing. In place of what his father will never say, Ken substitutes the revenge of power. His father can sell his stock. But money never quite makes up for what is missing. "To the day I die it is going to bother me. It is just like the play, 'I Never Sang for My Father.' "

There was one last story. For years Ken and Jack stayed up all night Christmas Eve, drinking and talking. Sometimes their father joined them. Occasionally, when Ken was not around, Jack and his father stayed up alone. One year Ken asked his father to stay up alone with him. "He wouldn't do it. Not with me. And I asked him, 'You've done this for years with Jack, why won't you stay up and...' 'Well, I'm getting too old for that....' He didn't really want me to know him the way that Jack knew him, or something."

Speaking intimately is terribly important, and risky, for Ken. Here it is tied directly to the damaged relationship with the father. Note how once again Ken reverses the vulnerability. Not "He didn't want to know me," but, "He didn't want me to know him." As is his habit, Ken turns himself into the threat, in order to deflect a bit the pain of rejection. He preserves an image of himself as predator in order to deny the wound of his father's disregard. Competitive success is what he has instead of his father's blessing. However, the substitution is poor recompense.

Once again, a description of his father-in-law provides us an indirect insight:

> I learned from him how much better off you are being a listener than a talker when you first get to know people. Now I'll sit back and not say anything until I find out what the other person is about.... I observed how effective that was.... The only way is to give a person the chance to expose themselves. If they are insincere or not interested in you, then why waste your time? But if they expose themselves as a sincere, loyal friend, then you should respond accordingly.

This passage can sound manipulative. It describes a strategy of listening: sit back, let the other guy expose a weakness. But it also suggests what Ken is reluctant to admit: how hungry he is for the intimacy he could never attain with his father, at the same time that he fears the emotional manipulation at which his father excelled. I said something along these lines to him, drawing the parallel between what he had said about his father and what he says of Mike. He agreed:

> Yes, it is the same situation with my Dad. I can do all this great stuff and he still doesn't recognize it.... You know, I would say it has been a very one-sided relationship. It's been more meaningful to me to be his mentor, to try to save this guy, than it has been for him to be saved.... I treated him as a friend, but not necessarily as an employee, and as a friend he has disappointed me miserably, miserably.... I guess that is why it gets me. I've given so much and gotten so little in return.

To sum up then, Ken has attempted to be for Mike what his own father has never been for him. Pushing aside his fear of self-exposure, Ken has attempted to be a confidant and a friend. But Mike has rebuffed the offer, manipulating Ken's self-exposure to his own advantage. Instead of making up for the painful history with the father, this relationship has reenacted it down to the last demeaning betrayal. Demoting Mike is partly an act of retaliation. Although Ken imagines Mike's "festering anger," he is remembering his own suppressed rage at his father. The harsh demotion—severing an arm or two— will at least ease this wound, whose memory Mike has evoked.

Of course, Ken does not say most of this, and might find it difficult to acknowledge. He casts the decision in terms of company policy. This too serves a defensive function. Aggression is Ken's first defense against wounded affection; the impersonality of business is his defense against acknowledging that any of this story matters to him personally. Ken's odd thought that his employees will be reassured, that they will now hasten to share their profiles with each other, now makes sense in terms of the restoration of impersonality. Just as he told me, "I don't mind talking to you because you are getting something out of it," he expects his employees to understand the difference between real self-exposure, which would be dangerous, and the controlled exposure of business. This distinction, which he needs to restore in order to save his pride, is what he expects his employees to understand as a matter of policy.

And perhaps they will. After all, for all that these events are intensely personal, they take place within a public culture that suppresses their personal significance. The self-misunderstanding Ken requires is not something idiosyncratic; it is "out there," in the shared language that makes work workable.

5

Public Lives and Private Motives

Clearly, Don and Ken start from different—nearly opposite—premises. Don begins by describing his need to separate sharply his life at home and at work. Ken starts from the opposite point, his conviction that "team spirit" is only possible if the manager and his players socialize after hours. On closer examination, these men have more in common than either might recognize. Each is struggling with the boundary between private and public life; each is highly ambivalent.

The problems Don and Ken face reflect simultaneously a real strain imposed by work and their own private, psychological sensitivities. Both men are in occupations that demand a high degree of interpersonal engagement. At the same time, the genuineness of that engagement is severely limited.

As a psychotherapist, Don is drawn into the most intimate secrets of other people's lives. Their stories evoke his own fantasies and anxieties. Yet if he is to serve them, he must retain his emotional distance. This is a strain that every clinician will recognize. As an administrator, Don has responsibility for running a newly created, disorderly organization. To be effective, he must keep his aggravation from making him testy with subordinates.

Ken practices a managerial style in which he becomes involved in his employees' lives. Certainly there are other styles. For some men, the code of impersonal pragmatism remains an ideal. Bob, a later case in this study, thinks business relationships should be fair, unemotional and impersonal. He imagines the good old days, when men of his father's generation could walk into the Ford plant and say, "I make a good machine part; I want your business." Today, Bob laments, everything is salesmanship.

Whether business practice in the good old days was ever as impartial as Bob imagines is questionable. Certainly it is no longer. "Judge me for what I can do, not for who I am," is too simple a slogan where personality is a calculated part of salesmanship or managerial competence. The ideal of impersonal pragmatism must now include the businessman's version of the bedside manner. At the same time, it must set certain boundaries. To be effective on the job, and even minimally comfortable with oneself, the technique of work friendliness must not be confused with genuine intimacy. Today, Ken is representative of one large current in business theology. For Ken to be effective, he, like Don, must draw a line between collegiality and emotional engagement.

Don's and Ken's experience of the strain also reflects their individual personalities. Don is afraid that if he gets too close to someone else he will become "part of their problem." The history of this fear—the strangled twin, the father's heart attack—is unmistakable. Ken is afraid that if he reveals himself to anyone he will be weakened and demeaned. This concern surfaces repeatedly; there are friends who betray confidences, business rivals who try to provoke an indiscretion. Most notable is his battle with Mike, a battle that recapitulates his disappointing relationship with his father.

The two men describe their solutions in curiously similar terms. Each mentions his sense of acting "in role." The idea of acting in role is a solution provided by the culture of work. It allows each man to address both the social and psychodynamic problem he faces. Socially, the sense of acting in role allows Don and Ken to give as much of themselves as the job demands, yet retain the distinction between work life and private life. Don trades roles— minister, psychologist, husband—and in this way leaves the cares of each occupation safely outside the door of the next. Ken invites his employees home, yet never loses track of the difference between colleagues and friends.

Psychodynamically, the sense of acting in role promises each man a resolution to his ambivalent wish to be wholly engaged and at the same time safely dispassionate. Don gets to feel that he can be wholly available (to his boss, his wife, his children) without worrying that his own private turmoil will invade the relationship and make him "part of the problem." Ken gets to socialize with his employees in the brotherly (or fatherly) fashion he longs for, without worrying that he will be drawn in too far, forced to lose his cool, and humiliated.

But if the idea of acting in role promises a solution, it is, for several reasons, a difficult one. First, it requires men to be self-consciously dispassionate. The strain of work relationships is that they must be both personal and reserved at the same time. The image of self-in-role rationalizes this expectation, but it also keeps the tension clearly—perhaps too clearly—in view.

Some men are reassured by this explicit distinction between real emotion and its calculated simulation. Ken, for example, is astonishingly explicit about the difference between genuine friendship and the limited collegiality of business. This makes him an effective informant—listening to him is like being shown behind the scenes by a master—but at the same time his deliberateness can be chilling. Similarly, Don describes his self-conscious emotional restraint in terms that can make a listener uncomfortable. For both of these men, the awareness of their own dispassion is reassuring. Ken feels that he will not be swept away in emotion as he once was by his father's outbursts. Don feels he will not impose his emotional demands on others as he fears he once did with disastrous results. But for most men, who are not as fearful of their emotionality, this sort of self-conscious restraint would not match psychodynamic needs, and would simply become fatiguing.

The second problem is that the idea of acting in role holds men to an ideal of impersonality that is almost impossible to maintain in practice. Don and Ken would both prefer to keep their private motives from invading their public performance. As we have seen, however, neither man succeeds in sustaining the boundary. Don suffers from "stress" and Ken becomes emotionally attached to his subordinates.

For two reasons, then, the ideal of acting in role is a demanding resolution. It keeps the dilemma of impersonal collegiality too explicitly in view, and it offers no time-out for relaxation. How do men deal with this rigorous code? Don and Ken illustrate two answers.

First, they absorb much of the strain themselves, disguising it is as best they can. Don tells us that he suffers from "stress," which he presents to us as a somatic experience. We understand "stress" to be his experience—and disguise—of the problem of impersonal collegiality. Ken does not seem to disguise the issue, but keeps it more clearly in view. Ken has worked out a code that allows him to distinguish real friendship from business relations. This code provides him some relief. But as we have seen, Ken talks about this distinction continually. His brother and father are not personal enough with employees; his father-in-law is a model of the personal manager. A subordinate of Ken's could not keep the boundary straight, and so had to be fired. (The fact that Ken fired this man is itself another example, Ken claims, that he *can* separate personal feelings from the unpleasant requirements of being a boss.) If Ken's code helps him explain how business should be conducted, his obsession with the idea suggests that he is always worried. When he describes meeting with the salesman who sells him machinery, who "puts the move on him," or the union representative who tries to provoke him, he tells us indirectly that he often feels on the verge of being dominated and demeaned.

The second way that men deal with the strain is to find outlets in the culture of work itself. Here, Ken is the best example. He has tried to become a mentor to Mike. Mentoring, an old practice that recent scholarship has suddenly brought to public attention, can be understood as a way that work culture provides a semi-institutional release from its own austere code. If business is supposed to be impartial and unemotional, relationships between mentors and protégés are built on favoritism and affection. Of course, if mentoring serves this function its standing within the culture is ambiguous.

Like red-light districts in large cities or speakeasies during Prohibition, the relief it offers from official virtue must always be unofficial and its tenure fragile. Ken's difficult relationship with Mike and his subsequent repudiation of that relationship in favor of official disinterest cannot be unusual.

The third possibility, the least demanding, is that men will be inconsistent. We might anticipate that whatever combination of psychodynamic and cultural defenses men settle on, it will be inherently unstable. We can expect there to be moments when men relax their vigilance, allowing themselves to acknowledge a bit more explicitly their attachment to each other. These moments of relaxation, we might predict, will be followed by disappointment and sudden, extreme refurbishing of the impersonal denial. Ken's relationship with Mike is an example of this cycle. Mike, however, seems to have been a rare exception in Ken's life. For other men, who use other career strategies, this cycle is a recurrent theme.

The next section presents three men who face a psychodynamic problem similar to Ken's, but who turn to a different cultural solution. Each begins by describing how much he enjoys the social aspects of his work. Mike, who operates a small store, pictures his sales staff as a warm, feisty family. Al, who sells real estate, explains that he really thinks of himself more as a counselor. Ben says that what he most likes about teaching is developing personal contact with his students. These initial descriptions recall the way Ken began; Ken too saw himself as the "coach" in his company. Continuing the parallel, it soon emerges that Al and Mike are each obsessed with issues of dominance and submission. Mike's attempts to be affectionate with his customers, his business associates or his children continually turn into wrestling matches in which absolute victory or crushing defeat are the only alternatives. Al, who attempts to become his boss's favorite son, feels humiliated when he is rejected. Ben does not exactly feel dominated, but his attempts to be personal eventually leave him feeling demeaned. Finally, each of these men turns to ambition as a way of restoring his damaged self-esteem. (Ben has some trouble on this score. He attempts to be ambitious, but for various reasons is inhibited. He ends up feeling alternately lonely, mediocre, and "bored.")

This cycle of attempted affection, humiliating rejection, and counterattack is common to Ken, Mike and Al. None of them acknowledges his personal sentiments. They differ, however, in their strategies of disavowal. For Mike and Al, career advancement becomes the vehicle of self-restorative aggression. Like the imagery of self-in-role, the image of career trajectory conceals beneath an ostensibly impersonal surface a subtext of highly charged interpersonal meaning.

As a disguise, career trajectory holds the advantage over self-in-role in that its interpersonal meaning is less explicit. Ken is very aware of the pain he is inflicting on his protégé. What he disguises from himself is his personal investment in revenge. In contrast, Al and Mike, through the medium of trajectory, deny altogether that what they are doing has interpersonal significance. Al, from whom we will hear next, describes his workaholic "energy." Mike likens his career path to a bullet's trajectory. Behind each of these terms lies an interpersonal referent: fears of rejection and self-diminishment. Ben is a little too aware of how much aggression lies behind his ambitiousness. In his reluctance to be ambitious, he shows us more directly what Al and Mike enact but do not avow.

The solution these men find is psychologically easier than Don's or Ken's. Career trajectory allows them a more thorough disguise of interpersonal meaning than does self-in-role. But trajectory only addresses the meanings of aggression, disguising its interpersonal significance behind the impersonal image of "energy." Trajectory leaves untouched the more affectionate side of work relationships. Up to a point, this may make the psychological task easier. Compared to Don and Ken, Mike and Al suppress less of the attachment they feel toward their co-workers. But to the degree that truly personal relationships are impractical in the workplace, these men end up sounding peculiarly naive and vulnerable.

Al, who makes a good living by being a very aggressive salesman, prefers to dwell on the personal concern he feels for his clients. Mike, who sometimes describes his store as a small corporation, would like to think of his employees, and maybe even his customers, as "family." Ben has a special, personal touch with his students. None of these men distinguishes between real affection and professional amiability. Instead, each operates as if work's semblance of intimacy were genuine. The predictable problem is that all of these men are vulnerable to recurrent disillusionment. Mike, in particular, seems to court disappointment. He attempts to establish personal relationships with unlikely partners: his staff and even his customers. At those moments of disappointment, each man abandons the attempt to be personal and restores his damaged stature through his own version of trajectory.

In some ways, then, the solution trajectory offers is psychologically less strenuous, allowing a more thorough disguise of interpersonal meaning than self-in-role. It also disavows the interpersonal meanings of aggression only, not those of affection. But this solution, more total in one sense, but more limited in another, has its own problems. By solving only part of the problem of work it lends itself to a cycle of impossible hopes, disappointments, and aggressive retreats.

Career trajectory and the awareness of acting in role are by no means mutually exclusive. Each is encouraged by the work culture, and each promises a solution to the social and psychodynamic strains to which men are vulnerable. Yet of the men presented here, only Ken seems to avail himself of both options. (Although I have not dwelt on this feature of Ken's story, his aggressive expansion of the business—a version of trajectory—is a way of demonstrating that he is a better man than either his belittling father or his brother.)

The other men in this study present a more limited picture. Don's concern with being nice prevents him from being as aggressive as he might be. Although Don has in fact risen to a position of some responsibility, he does not experience his career as a rising curve. His promotion does not satisfy his aggression, even in disguised form. Instead, he feels only the anxiety of finding himself in a new, unstructured situation. Al and Mike, whose stories appear next, exploit the disavowal of aggression offered by trajectory, but do not seem able to distinguish genuine attachment from its calculated appearance.

A final word about Ken may be in order: Ken's language, behavior, and (perhaps above all) his candor may make him sound brutal. I find for myself that the story he tells of his childhood makes him at least more understandable. More than that, compared to the more engaging but ultimately less realistic men who follow, he begins to appear remarkably well-suited to the demanding social situation in which he operates.

Part Three

The Trajectory of Careers

6

The Man No One Could Ignore

The idea that a career should describe a rising trajectory—each new job becoming, in its turn, a stepping stone to one with more responsibility, power, and salary—is probably strongest in large organizations. In corporations, hospitals, universities, and the military, the very structure of the organization, with its pyramidal layers of management, encourages this expectation. But the idea of career trajectory is not limited to these settings. Men who work in small offices, or even those who are self-employed, expect their careers to move forward. A small businessman cannot very well dream of becoming vice president, since the office does not exist in his setting, but he will find other ways to measure how far he has come.

The meaning of career trajectory is not at all obscure. It measures a man's aggressiveness, his energy, perhaps his competence; it describes what he has "made of himself." None of this requires interpretation. We do not need to investigate men's unconscious fantasies to know this; they will tell us directly. But there are other meanings connected with trajectory buried beneath what men are willing to acknowledge.

If trajectory addresses some of the same problems as the image of self-in-role, its great advantage is its disguise. Self-in-role makes the dilemma of personal relations in business explicit; trajectory conceals the issue behind an ostensibly impersonal surface. But trajectory has its own weakness. At some point, the rising curve of every career levels off. This leveling off is forced by social structure itself, the pyramid of opportunity narrowing as one advances until, for most men, only lateral moves are possible. At the same time, most men begin to lose their aggressiveness. Other interests, perhaps family, begin to take precedence over career building. For whatever combination of diminishing social opportunity and waning personal ambition, career trajectories begin to flatten out. At that point, even if it is in some measure welcome, the meaning of upwardness must be renegotiated. Both the pride in moving upward and whatever fear or pain were concealed behind it must find another symbolic vehicle.

Al Silver, age forty-one, can see that day not far ahead of him. Al made $90,000 last year selling real estate, and could probably keep that up indefinitely. Yet he feels that time is running short, that he needs to move on. The pressure of the Next Move is upon him. He expresses the compulsion he feels in terms of careerism. It will be our project to see what other meaning lies behind this formulation, and how the text of work disguises its latent significance.

Al has done very well at real estate. Money aside, he says, "I have become very much a part of the company for [which] I work. I assume I will own a piece of it shortly. Maybe not. I expect I will be offered a partnership this year."

This part is not true. Gradually Al let me know that he really has very little hope at all of ever becoming a partner. Spencer Ames, the owner of the company, is fifty-eight. Some day he may retire, but even then, Al knows, Spencer is not likely to leave Al any opening to take over. For all Al's success, Spencer mistrusts him. The problem has to do with Al's personal style. "Just emotionally he is offended by the intense way I relate to people personally. He is fond of everyone and close to no one. He is a ferocious tennis player; he can knock the shit out of someone half his age. But always . . . very clean. Tennis is a gentleman's game. You never hear an off-color comment, or a dirty word from Spencer. Never a raised voice; you rarely see him frustrated or angry."

If Spencer never loses control, however aggressive he may be underneath that courtly exterior, Al is an absolute geyser of emotion:

> I'm a workaholic. I need a work environment where I can extend myself eight, ten, twelve hours a day, six days a week. I just have massive energy. I'm a classic Type A, driven workaholic. . . . Also I need to provide for my self-indulgences, which are quite evident around the house. [Real estate] allows me to work as hard as I want and make as much as I want. I spend every bloody penny of it, frankly. I have a son here and a daughter at Bard, which is one of the most ferociously expensive colleges the little brat could have found. . . . I had to create stability [after leaving my marriage and another job] where it was wildly unstable, and do it while paying child support.

Al describes himself as a man of enormous, ungovernable appetites. Although he speaks in terms of money—and there is his characteristic defiance to "spending every bloody penny"—he makes clear that wild, disorderly emotion is what drives him. Massive debts and massive energy are both stabilized on rivers of cash and driven achievement. Sometimes Al suggests that his boundless aggressiveness is what made him a great salesman: "I could sell anything to anyone, and they loved me for it. I really loved the work; it was legitimized aggression. I got paid for what I used to get kicked in the ass for: being aggressive and stating my opinions." Yet it seems that Spencer does not really approve after all.

Sometimes Al suggests that he is not really a cutthroat salesman; it is his personal concern that makes him good. "I really see myself as a counselor. Oddly, or not oddly at all, I have always had a very strong relation with the academic community, with people who don't respond well to the used car types. I deal with a billion divorcées, widows... and I have a very strong influence within that kind of community."

The genuineness of Al's professed affection for his customers is suspect. I think it will become clear that he is far too egocentric for us to take this account literally. The widows and divorcées are bit players in a drama Al constructs. The main character he notices is himself. Still, this passage is important. It reveals the continuing debate Al holds with himself about what sort of man he is. Is he unsupportably aggressive, or is he genuine and personal? Interestingly enough, he calls both of these options by the same word. They are both examples of the way he is "emotional." Spencer, by contrast, is not emotional in either sense. He is never aggressive, at least not overtly, and according to Al, he is a pretty cold fish all the way around.

> Spencer does not have a good sense of the needs and expectations of the people who work for him.... It is reflected in his home life. His wife has reported to me with some pain that he wasn't much of a father. He found it difficult to relate to the needs of his daughters. He didn't see the connection between them and him, didn't take them very close to his heart. He ran them the way he runs business. Waitresses, daughters, they are all the same. A very distant man, covered up by this gentle, quiet demeanor....
>
> He respects me, but only as an employee. I have been working there six years. In that time, in most other companies, there would have been a closer business relationship. I have no more progress with him or trust than the day I started.

In these passages Al comes as close as he can to saying that what he needs from Spencer is something more personal than respect. He needs to feel that he has Spencer's blessing. Yet when I asked about this directly, Al backed away:

> *RO:*   Do you need anything from him personally?
>
> *A:*   Until now, no. He has given me everything I need: absolute freedom.... But what I need from him [now], that closeness, being the heir, is not there, and it is causing an irreparable separation. Not anger or bitterness; just if it is not there, I must then pursue it on my own.

It turns out that Spencer is not the first older man upon whose recognition Al's career has turned. When he first got into real estate there was a mentor, someone who presumably noticed the same raw energy that Spencer finds so offensive, but who recognized its potential. "He was very generous of himself, gave me a lot. When he hired me I had hair halfway down my back. I wore blue jeans and smoked cigars. I wouldn't have hired me on a bet. Not only [did he hire me], he gave a shit whether I succeeded. Told me when I was doing good and chewed me out when I made mistakes. Always with real affection."

Yet when I asked, "What do you think he saw in you?" Al replied:

> I don't know that he saw anything at first. I don't know if he had the brains to know a good agent from a bad one. He sure hired a lot of bums.... It was no great compliment that he took me. I was scuzzier than most. Now if you looked at the background, most of those bums had two years of college... if that, or thirty-seven years of failure behind them. If you really sat down and profiled me, I wasn't likely to fail in quite the same way.

So the question remains. Did this boss really recognize anything in Al? Was it the acknowledgment Al needs? Al remembers him with affection, grateful for the personal friendship that went beyond business. Yet the portrait Al draws of him holds a large measure of contempt: "He is forty-six, overweight, drinks too much. High school degree, maybe. Good salesman, blow-hard. Heart as big as the world, probably a liver to match it. Big ideas, small capacity to follow through on them."

Before him there had been another man. When Al graduated from college, a family friend "scribbled down a few names on a piece of paper." With this introduction, Al landed his first job as an editor. His first boss, "saw something in me that I didn't recognize. He offered me the opportunity to do something. He cared enough to ask from time to time how I was doing."

Still earlier, there was the story of how Al went to college in the first place. He had done a remarkably mediocre job of high school, barely graduating from a small school that sent only a quarter of its students to college. He applied only to Columbia, and at first was rejected out of hand. Then the college received his test scores, all in the middle ninetieth percentile, and suggested he come up for an interview, "which I did the next day. Just caught a train, walked in, said, 'I'm here; interview me.' And I was accepted two days later."

A pattern begins to emerge. At each step we see Al as a defiant young man. He didn't bother to work in high school. "I was never there on time, never raised my hand and never did any work." But he also mentions that he never missed a day of school past eighth grade. We can picture him waiting, stonily, for someone who will recognize the special spark. He approached Columbia in the same way: "Here I am; what are you going to do about it?" Would they notice—they almost did not—that he had something more going for him than his surly manner promised?

When recognition does come, Al is pleased, but yet still brusque. The family friend who made possible his first career as an editor, he says, did him no great favor; he simply scribbled down a name or two. His mentor in real estate cared for him, but he was probably too drunk to notice what a poor bet he was making.

The story that Al tells of his career is that, at several crucial moments, he has been discovered. He is a diamond in the rough—very rough. But at each critical juncture in his life—entering college, starting out in publishing, getting into real estate—someone took a closer look and saw the potential beneath the abrasive surface. Although Al disparages each of these incidents (he was accepted at college because his test scores were overwhelming, his letter of introduction was an indifferently scribbled name, his mentor was a drunk), it is clear how much he values these moments of recognition. He desperately wants Spencer to recognize him in somewhat the same fashion. But Spencer, it seems, is not going to come through. He will not extend himself; he will be put off by Al's truculence and never notice the potential beneath it.

It would be an exaggeration to say that Al cannot acknowledge the personal side of what he needs from Spencer. This is not for him an unthinkable thought, but it does make him uncomfortable. Faced with Spencer's coolness, Al finds it convenient to retreat to careerism: "I have done this thing, proved that I am awfully good at it. If I take myself seriously it is time to move on to the next thing.... I am living with the belief that I am supposed to be challenged at all times. That money is not a very good goal, it is a tool to something else, but that the real goal in life is some kind of development and challenge."

The options Al describes are revealing. He has considered joining a large real estate firm in New York or Washington. Here, success would be measured in amassing an enormous income. Al protests that the thought does not really excite him. He thinks he may be more the contemplative, bookish type than the aggressive sort who wants to "slug the shit out of everyone." Yet he also acknowledges, "I can be wildly competitive." If success is to be measured in money, Al could play that game with a will. He has also thought about going into competition with Spencer, trying, as he says, to "muscle him out." And then again, half joking, he says he might just sell the business, throw everything in the truck, and go live on the Navajo reservation in New Mexico. "Working in Chin Lee, or some other little speck on the map... Writing, perhaps simply good deeds if you will. A committed and dedicated life... one of a charitable, or rather a self-sacrificing, nature."

If Chin Lee is only a fantasy, it still catches us by surprise. It seems so utterly unlike everything else we have heard. Here is a man who earns a torrent of money every year and boasts about spending it self-indulgently, who seems to thrive on human contact, sometimes aggressive, sometimes nurturant, who seems obsessed by his boss's unwillingness to notice him, daydreaming about becoming a virtuous, impoverished hermit. He might even write, and so revive the scholar in himself. Although some people do manage to be humble, virtuous, poor and intellectual in places like Chicago, Al sees that future in terms of a "speck on the map." Clearly this business with Spencer, and whatever relation it has to Al's career trajectory, has set off some very powerful—and contradictory—fantasies.

One thing that Chin Lee represents is tranquility. This seems an odd attraction for a man who describes himself as "a classic Type A personality" with "massive appetites." Yet it turns out that there is another side to Al. At one point I asked how he came to return to graduate school. He said that he came upon an old Shaker dirge in a songbook that so moved him he became obsessed with American history.

> The music itself was terribly moving. And it kindled an interest that I'd had all along in community building. Not because I think they are great; I think they are a bunch of idiots, frankly. They are a pretty rough bunch toward each other. They are rigid and demanding, a rather humorless group. . . . There was something about the emotionalism of it that I found very appealing, though I can't come to terms with their rather pathetic philosophy, which was terribly humble. . . . I think in many regards they were very much at peace with themselves. Perhaps it was a sense that I don't have about myself; I am not at peace with myself. Certainly in joining the community they gave up all ambition. . . . I have a great fondness for tranquility that I don't have. I couldn't live with it either, to be honest. No way in hell. Fucking or no fucking [the Shakers were celibate], that is not the weakness. The weakness is that they had no will. And I've got plenty.

This long passage suggests a distinction that Al himself may not notice. The Shaker dirge, Al says, is emotional. It is specifically not emotional in the sense of willful energy, but rather in a way that leads to tranquility and human closeness. This experience of community and peace is exactly what the other side of Al's emotionality—his aggression—prevents him from achieving. Yet, characteristically, no sooner does he say this than Al is back to disparaging the Shakers as coldhearted spinsters—a lot like Spencer. Al could never live like them; he has too much will. Once again, willfulness is the way he denies wanting the human warmth that the Shakers represent, except, he quickly adds, they are not really giving at all.

In his description of the dirge, the idea of tranquility leads Al quickly to community. This too is one of the potential attractions of a small town like Chin Lee. Al is fascinated by the question of how people build communities. He has an extensive collection of plat books, the old records that document who owned the parcels of land in Ingham County generations ago. He knows the history of local ethnic groups and manufacturing concerns, now represented only in the names of their descendants. Why does he study these things? Al answers in terms of community: "I am talking about how people organized their lives. A mill or a factory is simply an organization of people. Somebody had to decide to build miniature motor parts and hire other people, and they built a community around it."

Al's notion of community focuses on collective enterprise, on the things people can do for each other. When he thinks of Chin Lee, he imagines a life of "simple good deeds," "charity," and "self-sacrifice." The Shakers, he says, gave up all ambition. Small midwestern towns started with commercial ventures, but these were the nucleii around which communities grew. Each of these descriptions implicitly contrasts commercial ambition with collective good. It sounds as if Al is explaining something about his own life. Here is a man who self-indulgently "spends every bloody penny" that he makes by aggressive salesmanship. Yet, as we have heard, sometimes Al seems to be saying that he has made Lansing his community, his theater for virtuous commerce. He speaks of himself as "a counselor," and suggests that he has a strong influence within the academic community. But of course he would find it difficult to stay with so pacific a conception of himself very long. A bit later he remarks that he feels very much an outlander in Lansing, an East Coaster who calls himself "a snob from the word go." He thinks Lansing has no community spirit. He despises the social service activism that animates local politics and suggests that what this town needs is more parades and public statuary.

One thought that Al has about retiring to a place like Chin Lee is that he might write, picking up an abandoned career. Al is a scholar, and in particular a writer, manqué. In college he discovered a passion for books. On graduating he became an editor and then became fascinated with printing and bookmaking. These days he collects old books; his collection of plat books is the most extensive in the county.

Sometimes Al contrasts his present occupation with the "pretentious" academic life he has left behind. When we first met, he began by telling me how much he disliked academic types. "There is a pervading sense of superiority, which I suppose I was once guilty of myself. It seems to be based on job security and poor pay, which one has to compensate for one way or another. In any society the shamans, intellectuals, craftsmen are set apart, looked at as being strange, mystical, or just damn weird."

(Based partly on this antagonistic beginning—since I am one of those poorly paid, presumably condescending academics—partly on the bored, truculent tone of its delivery, and partly on the fact that Al had not arrived for our first scheduled interview, I offered to stop before either of us wasted our time. Warily, we agreed to continue. From here the interviews took a surprising turn. Though Al remained truculent to the end, he also became more personal than most of the men I interviewed. I eventually came to understand that that odd combination of chip-on-the-shoulder disparagement and personal warmth is the heart of his dilemma.)

At other times, Al suggests that real estate has its own store of knowledge. "I have given myself more serious training [in real estate] than a college major gets. I have had between 700 and 900 hours of serious professional schooling of some sort." He added, "The intellectual challenge appeals to me, and helping others."

The fantasy of retiring to Chin Lee, however unrealistic it is, seems then to pull together a constellation of themes that are diametrically opposed to Al's current career, although they are surreptitiously represented in real estate as well. How did Al come to divide his world in this way? This is the history he told: Both of Al's parents were highly educated people, well known and admired in the Washington intellectual circles in which they moved. They were, he says, "genuinely respected and humble people." They were also politically committed people: both were members of the American Communist Party. His mother was a professor of English at Georgetown University, his father a musicologist and art historian of whom Al tells anecdotes that border on the fantastic. "He could look at a print and tell you if the color was right on it. Had he never seen the original, he would tell you if the color was right or wrong. . . . I watched him identify a piece of music he had never heard. He said, "It has got to be this." He once drove a music contest off the air. He won it every day for four weeks. Godawful obscure music, snippets. . . . "

Al tells another story, intended to illustrate his father's deep, emotional involvement in music.

> There is a wonderful story. The Library of Congress has six Stradivari instruments, played by a quartet in residence. For years and years my father sat in the fourth row on Friday night and listened to the Budapest quartet play those magnificent instruments. He'd sit there and they would sit there. . . . One day he passed one of the violists, Boris Kroyt, walking in Dupont Circle. I don't know if you know, Dupont Circle is a very ritzy place. And my father knew who Kroyt was; he had been staring at him for twenty-five years. But Kroyt had been staring back at my father for twenty-five years too; they had grown old together. And they said hello to each other, and became, not close friends, but developed a passing acquaintance over having been so close as it were. My father, that is the way he was with music: very personal.

The anecdote is intended to describe the father's depth of feeling, yet it strikes a slightly off-key note. Kroyt and Al's father have stared at each other for twenty-five years, they have grown old together, they are both lovers of fine music, yet when they finally do greet each other they become "passing acquaintances." Somehow we might have expected more. As Al tells it, what is emotional in the experience remains wrapped up in the music. The two men nod, and pass on.

Not only is the encounter between Kroyt and the father meager, there is something peculiar about the rest of this description. Al dwells more lovingly on those violins than the music they produce. This too reminds us of something. In a curious way, Al has always seemed more fascinated by the artifacts of community than the actual experience. He loves Shaker music, but despises the people who wrote it. He collects land records of Ingham County, but never actually feels that he belongs to the community. He thinks the town needs less civic activism and more monuments. He loves printing, but is often contemptuous of scholarship. Printing, land contracts, public monuments and now violins—they are all of a piece. They are the physical material, but not the spirit, of community.

Al, as we have come to see, has very mixed feelings about how close he wants to get to others. The picture he draws of his parents is far less ambivalent. In the anecdote of Kroyt and his father, he attempts, with less than total success, to portray his father's emotionality. More often he says directly what the story implies.

His father, he said, was "a hopeless old skinflint, tighter than hell." His parents had a stormy marriage that by all the evidence left its mark on both Al and his sister. We do not know what the fights were about. In fact, Al first said that he did not remember them at all. He knew only what his mother had told him: that her husband mistreated her, and that he was infuriatingly stingy. This idea of stinginess—referring at times to money, at other times to emotion—runs through his description of his entire family. Al's mother accuses her husband of stinginess. She herself was tight with money and affection: "She was a very dour woman, sour even. She came out of childhood with the name Mary Sunshine, and the corner candy store operator called her Bubbles. Well she was old sour puss herself. [The nicknames were given her in mockery.] Her hair was always pulled back. She never wore fancy clothes, or good clothes. Never treated herself as female."

His grandmother, Al claims, "was an eccentric old shit, incapacitated by terminal miserliness." His sister "gives a ton of presents and then takes them back. She uses gifts as a weapon of some sort." As an afterthought he adds, "It is funny, because in many ways she is a very tender woman, very sensitive. She has an eye for shape and form; very expressive. It's a very energetic part of her.... [However,] there is no warmth to her at all. Cold as ice. Her warmth is superficial."

This is a surprising juxtaposition of ideas. His sister is a miserly old witch, but she has a sensitive eye for art. We have heard him say the same of the Shakers: cold-hearted spinsters who wrote the most moving music. The same odd combination describes his mother. Although she is a "sour" woman who cannot buy clothes that would make her look feminine, "She was a very sensitive, intense woman."

This series of contrasts also, of course, includes the father: a fellow who could form a deep, emotional bond with music, but not with the man who played it, nor, we suspect, with his family. In each of these descriptions it seems that Al is worrying a puzzle. Who are these people in his family? Do they have blood in their veins or not? They seem to be passionate in some ways, yet whatever it is they care about, they never quite seem to care about *him.* And so it comes about that for Al, scholarship and artistic sensitivity are peculiarly loaded ideas. They are connected to the puzzle of his family's apparent sensitivity and actual emotional stinginess. At one point, Al said he felt that his father always disapproved of him. Why? "I was expected to be a good student and I hated the stuff. Expected to be diligent and save every nickel, and I never saved a goddamn penny." He still doesn't, because he, unlike his father, his mother, his sister—or Spencer—is a man of passion.

At first he said he did not recall the fights between his parents. Later he acknowledged living in fear of his father.

> He was not a good father to me. In my early years he was critical and bad-tempered. I never saw him much and when I did there was a lot of emotion involved, rarely any of it any good. In addition there was bitter competition between me and my sister. My father openly and clearly sided with my sister.... My mother and I were very close. But in younger years I don't have a real clear memory of my mother. Much more my father, because I was afraid of him. I wasn't beaten, but chased. I had all the signs of an emotionally abused child: bed wetter until into my early years, asthma, hay fever, extreme tension, lack of attentiveness.

He was afraid of the dark, and of dogs. "The popular dogs of the day were very assertive: boxers and high-strung poodles. A whole bunch of them, and I was always a paperboy. I got bit in my work frequently.... Nobody thought those dogs were biting kids. You were afraid of them and nobody did anything about it. Part of life. I got bitten all the time. And I didn't like accosting people. I never had any fear, but being confident enough to hit someone back is another story."

This passage suggests a side of Al's experience that we have not heard before. Over and over Al tells us how aggressive he is. Now it turns out that as a child he was fearful and unassertive. He was afraid of dogs, other children, the dark—and his father. Could it be that his defiance as an adult makes up for his childhood timidity?

The other interesting line in this passage is, "You were afraid, and nobody did anything about it." This idea matches other things we have heard him say. Nobody notices; the people in charge are not paying attention, not taking care. We have heard this theme all through Al's description of his adult career. A mentor notices something special, goes a little out of his way to take an interest—or maybe not, maybe he would have done as much for anyone.

These fragments of childhood memory are far from a complete history. But limited as they are, they begin to fill in the meaning of Al's career and the choice that now faces him. Al's career history now appears to divide between two opposite paths. On one side is the route that led him to graduate school and then publishing. This road is an attempt to capture some of his parents' virtuousness. Like his mother, he would become a scholar; later, like his father, a facilitator of other people's creativity. At one point in his life Al even mimicked his parents' political activism. As he puts it now, contemptuously, "I wore a lot of funny clothes and marched around . . . crusading for every stray dog."

In contrast, the decision to leave publishing and go into real estate was a way of thumbing his nose at everything his parents valued. Where they were abstemious he would be a spendthrift. Where they were devoted to political causes, he says "Now I have more personal goals. I am devoted to career advancement." Where they were self-effacing, he would be strident. Where they were cold, he would be a volcano of emotion. Where once he felt that nobody in charge paid attention (and this may be what he can least forgive), he is now impossible to ignore.

With it all, he has never quite given up on them. He won't say this at first—the first things he says are designed to shock—but after a while we learn that selling real estate contains a particle of what he claims to have left behind. He remains a bit the student, a bit the public servant.

And so we come to Spencer. If Spencer would make Al his partner, then these two opposite strands of Al's career might at last come together. Al would feel recognized and accepted as he has never felt at home. He would feel that his "emotionality" has been put in the best possible light, that he is someone who wants to be close to people—his widows and divorcées—not someone who has to beat people up. He would be rewarded with the respect, and perhaps even tranquility, of this midwestern community.

But if, as seems likely, Spencer refuses him, then the longed-for fusion of these opposite paths will break apart. Looking ahead to that time, Al can see only exaggeratedly opposite options. There is the road to New York: more money, more aggression, less peace. Or there is Chin Lee. In Chin Lee he might find the tranquility and the community he partly wants. But his description of the place—a speck on the map—tells us what he fears might be true of himself as well: that without his drivenness, his gargantuan appetite, he might fade from everyone's notice. Perhaps, he thinks, that would really be best after all. Live a life of virtuous simplicity, help the Navajo, maybe write his memoirs. His parents might have done something like that. But then the old meat eater comes charging back. He is going to muscle Spencer out of the business, slug the shit out of the boys in New York, make a ton of money and spend it all the next day.

There is a striking parallel between Al's story and Ken's. Both men describe their fathers as alternately enraged and emotionally distant. Although neither speaks comfortably of his own fearfulness, we gather from passing allusions that each was frightened by his father's capacity for rage. In self-defense, each man has, as an adult, made a point of establishing his own aggressiveness. Both men also feel that they were never able to establish as close a bond with their fathers as they would have liked. Each has attempted to create an improved version of that unsatisfying relationship with a colleague. They differ slightly in how they do this. Ken has attempted to reverse the generations, offering Mike what his own father could never offer him. In Al's case, the original order of generations is preserved: he wants Spencer (and the other incarnations who have preceded him) to make up for what his father failed to provide. Finally, both men have been notably unsuccessful in this attempt. The substitute actors that they have called in to play these old, familial parts have reenacted the piece with all too much fidelity. Instead of improving the past, Ken and Al have relived it. Ken ends up feeling demeaned by Mike, just as he once did by his father; Al ends up feeling that Spencer is every bit as emotionally abstemious and judgmental as his own father.

At this point the two men diverge. Ken returns to his official policy, "Business relationships are not really personal." Al, on the other hand, does not have such a policy. This does not at all mean that he is more open to personal relationships at work than Ken. All along we have heard how much trouble he has with them. Each time he starts to feel close to people he immediately disparages them. The difference between Al's way of managing his discomfort with affection and Ken's way is that Ken has an official policy of disinterest, Al does not. Al never denies the fact that he has strong feelings about the people with whom he works. His problem is that those feelings switch back and forth from unrealistic hope to unbearable disappointment.

Looking at the matter from a more social perspective, we might describe the difference between Al and Ken this way: Ken's solution is more conservative. Faced with the assault on his stature that Mike poses, the idea of acting in role restores Ken's sense of balance. It is no doubt a tense balance; we wonder how long it will last before the next exception appears. But it is stable at least in the sense that Ken returns to the position he held before Mike upset him.

In contrast, Al's approach seems to entail more extreme cycles of hope and disappointment. There is even a suggestion that Al has dealt with similar disappointments in the past by switching careers. In graduate school he found himself working for a professor who was "one of the coldest guys you'll ever meet," and so Al dropped out of the program. His career as an editor ended when he took off for an unannounced, week-long vacation—a characteristically defiant move—and was promptly fired. Each time, he moved to a new career that offered more direct scope for aggression and that, not insignificantly, was less scholarly. If he ends up moving to New York, he will continue this series.

If, then, Ken's solution restores him to where he began, Al's style of counterattack keeps him moving on. Up to a point, this has been a good thing for him. Career movement is, as we know, a virtue in this culture. But there are certain dangers on the horizon. What will happen when Al can no longer move up? Or when he no longer needs to, at least for reasons he can admit? Interestingly enough, the problem will be sharpened in a couple of years, when Al's two children graduate from college. At that point he will no longer need to be a cash factory. Looking ahead, he says, "I really don't know how I will respond in two years, when the responsibility ends. . . . I really am very unsettled." What will be meaningful when income alone is not a justifiable goal? Al has reduced his sense of purpose, a complicated and conflictual idea in his life, to trajectory. What will he do when trajectory is no longer plausible?

7

The Man Who Could Not Stop

In the fall of 1982, Michael Doyle, the owner of Green's Furniture in Niles, Michigan launched a Dutch auction. On Monday every item in the store was reduced ten percent, on Tuesday twenty percent, and so on. By Friday evening, when the last half-priced hide-a-bed left the bare showroom, Green's had lost $50,000. Additional heavy losses were anticipated, since there was no stock and insufficient funds to resupply for the Christmas rush. Mike boasted that the sale had been a triumph of publicity, but by March he had closed the doors.

The sale was a miscalculation. It was intended to restore Green's fading popularity, a point that bears further examination, but it overshot the mark. Why then did Mike not call it off, say on Wednesday, when the tidal proportions were already evident? Did he consider stopping, or perhaps simply withdrawing some merchandise for the next week's business? His answer is equivocal.

> *RO:* Did you consider calling it off?
>
> *M:* Well, I called my lawyer. We could legally close the store because we were over the fire limitation.... We considered it.

Moments later, however, Mike denied that he had ever seriously considered halting the sale.

> *M:* I wouldn't even think of [halting it], not in my wildest imagination.... My concern was that we could have a mob.
>
> *RO:* Did you discuss with your lawyer whether you could use the safety regulation as an excuse to close the store to save money?
>
> *M:* No, that was not my consideration. I did not think about anything related to money at all.

Perhaps he had no choice but to continue. Perhaps, in the thick of things, he lost track, the sale did not actually start costing him money until Thursday.

In any case, the financial details are less revealing than his explanation. Mike's reason for going on is not financial at all. He explains that midway through the sale he became aware of its "evil connotation" in people's minds. Many customers assumed that the store was going out of business. In order to combat this assumption, Mike felt that he had to carry through the sale no matter what the cost.

Whatever else may be said about this explanation, taken on its own businesslike terms it is illogical. Only a man who is in fact going out of business would sell all of his stock at less than cost. Anyone who intended to stay afloat would hold some merchandise for the next week's customers. If business was not the point, what was?

What is striking about the sale is its imagery of momentum. Once started, there is no turning back. Each day the prices drop lower, the crowds grow, the excitement builds. By the end, Mike reports, "Those people were panic-buying." It is an odd thought. His customers might well have been gleeful, but it is Mike's imagination that turns the cheerful chaos he created into a boiling mob.

This image of being caught up in a wave of mounting excitement runs throughout Mike's history. The sale reenacts in microcosm the large patterns of his career. If we examine his vita we discover the suppressed emotional significance of a drama whose only representation, at this point, is the imagery of momentum itself.

The dominant theme of Mike's career has been high velocity conquest. Occasionally we hear the other side of his mania—he loses enthusiasm and drops out. Once or twice he has tried to retire, but soon he is back to building empires. His rueful acknowledgment of this compulsion is less convincing than his obvious pleasure in the excitement.

He started college with the intention of finishing four years' work in three years. When he fell short, he quit. Interestingly, Mike says, "I was ahead of the schedule that might have been expected, but I was behind my own." Yet it turns out that Mike had completed barely more than average in his three years. Not only did he turn school into another high velocity challenge, and quit when he fell short, the story he tells now denies how ordinary his pace really was. Describing this period, Mike says:

> I will get into something very often and become disenchanted, lose sight of my own direction or the challenge, or just stagnate. . . .
> The courses at first would be a challenge, but inevitably I would get ahead of them, to where they would bore me. I would burn out too quickly. I'd attack them. . . . I'd be too far ahead, waiting for the rest of the class to catch up. I have always been extremely aggressive in that respect. Always went in with a full head of steam, like a bullet fired into the air. It takes off like a banshee, but eventually it reaches its apogee and that's it. It runs out of steam and just falls down.

Mike recognizes that this has been his pattern not just in school, but throughout his career. His own explanation—that he gets so far ahead he gets bored—is not really believable. Mike was certainly no academic superstar. A better clue lies in the word "attack." Mike does fine as long as he can see himself as a bullet. He loses interest when he is forced to march at the same step as everyone else: "If someone had told me I could finish high school in three years, I probably would have tried to do it sooner. But since I had to be there four years come hell or high water, it just didn't seem to do a thing for me." Velocity itself is the value in Mike's life.

His first major job after school was as a sales engineer for Pratt-Whitney. Mike found himself flying all over the country, instructing major companies how to use the measurement standards Pratt-Whitney had pioneered. He was a high-powered salesman who burned up his expense account fast enough to keep in constant trouble with his boss. But he was good; eventually the company offered him the manager's position of a new division. Mike turned it down. Now he says the pressure was too high, the pay too low, he wanted time with his family. Perhaps those were the reasons. He also said, "Part of it was the money, part that I was just no longer enjoying the corporate philosophy. They really had turned Milque-toasty. They were slowly but surely turning away from being an established world leader." For a time, Mike explained, Pratt-Whitney set the standard of measurement precision, and the world listened. Now the company was paying more attention to profit. Other technology companies were moving ahead. Once more, Mike was getting restive.

Several jobs later Mike started his own company selling industrial pipe systems. He prospered, eventually merged with a larger company, then quit when the board of directors refused to support him in a union battle. Summing up that portion of his career, Mike says,

My achievements have not been easy victories.... When I built the piping company, for most people it would have been enough to just build a successful company. To others, enough to merge it with a larger organization. Or another step further, to be given responsibility for a whole corporation. That wasn't enough for me. I had to have the whole everything, and let everyone else sit back and clip their coupons.

Green's Furniture was to have been Mike's final retirement from a business career marked by headlong acceleration. In the fifteen years since Mike left college, a year short of his degree, he has tried his hand at a dozen occupations. He has lived in the fast lane of corporate management, owned franchises, and started at least two businesses of his own. In everything he has done until now the mood has been aggressive expansion.

By contrast, Green's was an old-fashioned store in Niles, a rural town in southwestern Michigan. Mike loved the old-timey atmosphere, and dug out the old photos of the store from the 1920s to adorn his office. Nevertheless, when I first turned on the tape recorder, Mike began, "Green's is a typical corporate structure. I am the president of the corporation. I have two principal managers. The store is divided into three distinct departments. I typify myself as being chief clerk and bottle washer."

Is he chief bottle washer or corporate president? There is a part of Mike that would like to retire to gentleman farmer, but the rhythm of the corporate fast lane is in his blood. This is the part that admits no retreat.

Now it seems that Mike's ruinous sale is yet another instance of his expansive style. From the perspective of an outsider it seems reasonable to ask why he did not call a halt to the sale midway through. Mike of course has an answer, couched in the logic of business. It may really be that he could not have called the sale off, or even that he did not notice how large a loss was building. The facts of the matter—what he could have done, what he actually considered at the time—are lost to us. All that we have now is Mike's retrospective explanation. That explanation does not make sense on its own terms. What it suggests instead is that Mike somehow became trapped in his own sense of trajectory that admits no middle ground. The choices were either to plunge ahead or else, like the bullet, to fall to ground spent.

What is the meaning of movement in Mike's career? The portrait he paints of himself leaves little doubt: he is the Napolean of business. When Mike first worked for Pratt-Whitney he had all the authority of the world's leading company in measurement technology behind him. "We were world leaders. The amount of respect for the products we produced was just mind-blowing. I could go in and just bring a corporation the size of Bendix to an absolute standstill, just on my word. . . . I'd just tell them to shut the whole production line down. And their expenditures were absolute millions of dollars, just on my word."

In Mike's account the theme of authority and dominance emerges frequently. To hear him tell it, the world is populated by craven older men who alternately hamper his ascent and fear his boldness. At Pratt-Whitney, "The managers over me felt fairly threatened. I recognized that and enjoyed it, relished it." Speaking of the larger corporation with which he merged his piping company, Mike says, "The bastards were not going to let me own any more [stock in the company]; they were scared to death of me."

Recently he has been casting about for a new location for his store. For a while a deal seemed all but final; at the last moment the owner of the new building changed his mind. "For him to extricate himself from that lease with the previous occupant would have required some reasonably intelligent manipulation on his part. I feel maybe he just didn't have the resources. . . . I think he just crayfished. Pretty typical of people I have seen in business;

second generation money. The Daddy made all the money and they just manage it. That's a sorry testimonial."

Early in his career Mike went through a management training course. He scored exceptionally high on the final evaluation—so high, he says, that his supervisor in the company became intimidated. "He tried to make my position demeaning. I would not let him get a rise out of me. He would try to embarrass me in front of clients. I consider him a shallow man. . . . He ended up kind of a pathetic ass. Had I considered him more of a threat I would have gotten angry."

This last passage brings us to an interesting point. Mike does not often walk away from a battle, especially when the issue is humiliation. This incident, like his occasional attempts to retire, is an exception. It is not alone, however.

Seven years ago Mike and a partner started yet another corporation. The details of this venture need not concern us, although one aspect will sound familiar. The company was part of a pyramid sales organization. Pyramid organizations have since been ruled illegal in Michigan and many other states, since they prey on the same gullible, ambitious expansiveness as chain letters. Not surprisingly, Mike found the idea "intriguing" and bid for the franchise for the entire state of Michigan.

Reluctantly, he agreed to divide the state with a partner. Eventually the two quarrelled, parted, and met again a year later. Over lunch the ex-partner became abusive. "I've always enjoyed humiliating you," he said. Words led to blows; soon the two men were grappling in the alley behind the restaurant. Here Mike's story takes an interesting turn: "He wouldn't quit. I stopped in the middle. We were both in suits, and I am cut to shreds in the glass, and I started laughing at the ridiculousness of two businessmen fighting. I started to walk away. He grabbed me, said he was going to kill me. That was when I got mad. Up until then I was not mad. Right then and there I really beat the shit out of him."

With both his boss and his ex-partner, Mike tried to avoid the fight. There is something he knows about himself, captured in his phrase, "I would not let him get a rise out of me." The point is that Mike is vulnerable to being swept away. Occasionally he evades the fight, more often he ends up battling furiously. Once again we hear the power of momentum. Mike becomes caught up in the wave, crowing his domination, denying to the world his fear of humiliation.

We can say something more. Very often Mike himself is the provocateur of emotional reaction. He is the one who needles insistently. At one point I asked whether he had ever considered joining with the other small merchants in common cause against the shopping centers that menace every downtown businessman. He replied, "They are not my peer group. Surprisingly few businessmen are open and honest about what their problems are. I'm an open book; you pinch me, I yell. If I were involved in a group I would want to get right in under their goddamn skin and make them bloody mad, realizing what is happening, and that there are things we as a merchants group can do about it."

In a strikingly similar passage Mike describes his trouble getting through to his eldest son. "All I want to see is a minor chink in the armor.... You cannot put an old head on young shoulders; I know, my Dad couldn't with me. But I am one thing my Dad never was. I am truly emotional about it; I truly care. Just to cause a single chink, or oscillation, to cause him to go from this nebulous gray area he is living in."

When Mike held his sale he remarked that people in Niles did not seem to notice that he was in business. He was going to break down their indifference by "gently hitting them in the teeth." He continued, "We'll see if we can't elicit more of a response from people. We'll get them, erode away; eventually we will crack that facade that you have and get right down into your hot little buttons; make you recognize what it is that we are."

Two points stand out in these passages. The first is Mike's emphasis on emotional acknowledgment. The second is that human contact turns so quickly into a battle. The two are virtually inseparable. Mike would make people mad, hit them in the teeth, break down their resistance. Early in our interviews he described the family atmosphere of his store, saying, "We bicker and gnarsh and goof around."

Mike's speech is heavily seasoned with colloquialisms, some of his own invention. To my ear "gnarsh" and "nizzle"—as in his phrase, "nizzle someone in the ass"—sound vaguely Yiddish, and convey the warm but feisty emotionality I associate with Jewish families. Maybe Mike makes the same association. In any case, the context of these words makes clear the close connection Mike finds between emotional warmth and affectionate battling. As a last example, Mike and his sons, who are now fifteen and sixteen, wrestle. "Oh yeah, we wrestle, right down on the floor.... Those are real important. It doesn't require verbal communication; it's an association. They can kind of gauge their growth, their strength, against their Dad, and do it in a semicompetitive but very loving way." Always, it seems, the warmth of affection is expressed in some form of mock battle. Mike batters at people as if to say, "I am here; you cannot get away from me."

These last passages offer us a more precise picture of Mike's imagery of motion. He is obsessed not with simple velocity, but with acceleration. The sale, we noted, ran at an ever-quickening tempo. Now we hear the same refrain: emotionality quickens inescapably into struggle. I am suggesting that Mike's career is the theatrical vehicle for an imagery of acceleration, whose meaning concerns emotional acknowledgment and domination. For reasons we do not yet understand, emotionality is transmuted into a power struggle. Mike himself does not understand this. He may not even recognize it, though his occasional, short-lived attempts to retreat suggest a distant recognition of his fatal compulsion. It remains for us to discover the unconscious scenario, whose representative is now acceleration itself.

Childhood

The themes of Mike's adult career—his provocative insistence on emotional acknowledgment, his obsession with dominance and humiliation—have their source in his childhood experience. In these memories we also find the significance of acceleration. The story centers on his father.

The father Mike recalls was a jealous, insecure man with an explosive temper. He turned minor oversights into insults, and occasions for compassion provoked only his phenomenal anger. "How was he with you as a child?" I asked.

> An absolute tyrant, and I would never knuckle under. The combination was nitro and glycerin. Until I was eight or nine he would get me up in the middle of the night and beat the living shit out of me; kick me out of bed and make me sleep on straw. He would tell me if I was going to conduct myself like an animal I would sleep like an animal. . . . He would wake me up, find that the bed was wet, beat the living crap out of me and make me sleep on straw. Defiance, whatever his philosophy was, whatever reason I was wetting the bed, he felt that was an instance that I was not trainable. And his capacity to understand, be compassionate, whatever is necessary, was not there.

Looking back now, Mike prefers not to remember his own terror and shame. The beatings were not so bad; he probably earned them with his own devilishness. In any case, they were more frightening for his mother than himself: "His approach was just shattering, not so much to me but to my mother. She will never forgive him. Other than the fact that she is a very compassionate woman, in a couple of instances she probably could have killed him. Ninety-nine percent of the beatings I deserved. . . . I covered a lot of territory when I was a kid."

Our clue to how humiliated he must have felt comes indirectly. Parenthetically, after a long account of his hellion credentials, Mike acknowledges, "Surprisingly, through grade school and midway through high school I was one of the smaller boys in the school. I had altar boy looks: platinum blond hair and blue eyes, and maybe I looked like a pushover type. The undercurrent was that I was [here he started laughing] an interesting kid. There wasn't any kid who covered more ground than I did."

In another passage he describes his brother. "As a kid he was a wimp; the sickliest kid you ever saw. I don't know how many times I used to want to pound his daylights out. I never could; it was an absolute no-no in our house."

Why, we might wonder, did this sickly brother so enrage Mike, unless Mike saw in him a reflection of his own fervently denied, despicable weakness?

Mike recalls that his faher was not only terrifying when angry, he was an easily jealous man. "The family would be talking in the kitchen, and people would be having a sandwich, and he wouldn't be offered one. He wasn't even in the room. And we would have a war, I mean a war. 'Doesn't anyone like me around here?'"

A father who sees insult everywhere will be a hard man to love. As an adult, Mike says, he has come to feel closer to his father. "I really enjoy him now. I will do my damnedest to cajole him away from his areas of trigger mechanisms. He has mellowed some, and I probably have more. Of course I am quite secure in the things I do, so he is no challenge to me; I am the challenge to him. I have been able to shove my light under a bushel basket and look at him for what he really is: my Dad, the grandfather of my two boys."

This passage may be something of a sentimental exaggeration. At other times Mike acknowledges his continuing frustration. Try as he will, there is no getting through. There is no acknowledgment of affection on his father's part.

> He never really knew how to love. . . . He doesn't have a friend even in the family. And he doesn't realize that I am the only friend he has got. I really love my Dad, even though I consider him a classic prick. I love him for what he is: the only Dad I'll ever have. . . . He doesn't recognize that. He recognizes me as a challenge; I am a reasonably successful businessman. I try to tell him, "Maybe you didn't do all you wanted, but there are some good things. A daughter, two sons doing the best they can. . . . " I can tell him to his face that I love him, not for what he has done, but for what he is—my Dad—and I can't get that through his fucking head.

It may be that as an adult Mike became more forgiving of his father, more willing to avoid the pitched battles. We know that there is a sentimental side to him, a side that would rather be a family man than corporation president. We also know how easy it is for headlong ambitiousness to overtake him. Mike shares his father's penchant for turning affection into a battle.

As a child, Mike was in no position to be understanding or forgiving. He became a rebel. Even now, his eyes light up when he describes the crescendos in the running war his gang fought with the police.

> They were building a new police building. They were all on the first floor; we got up to the third floor and, lo and behold, what is up there but a great big double-doored safe. I said, "Come on, let's get this thing moving." We pushed it right through the fucking wall. It was too big to go through the window. That sucker went right through the brick wall, down three flights, through the friggin' sidewalk. The cops came roaring out the front door; we went out the back.

The war with his father came to a head when Mike was sixteen.

> I had come home late. He got on my case. He was going to kick my butt, and I said, "Don't, don't kick my butt; I've had enough." Which for my Dad is just like smacking him in the face with a stick. He just defied me, and I finally knocked him down. I didn't hit him, I tripped him. And I sat on him, and told him, "You know I could just punch the living shit out of you." And I left home. Once I got to the point where I realized I could hit him back, it was time for me to leave.

Let me go back to the image of the safe rocking back and forth, gathering momentum, finally crashing into glorious destruction. We have heard this before. It is the same imagery of mounting excitement and explosion that pervades Mike's career path. Now we begin to see its significance.

This is a scene Mike played with his father, how many times we can only guess. There are two aspects to it: first, Mike's sense that affection is never forthcoming because the father is too engrossed in his own perpetual injury; second, the pattern of turning emotion into something explosive. These days Mike denies how frightening that sequence really was, but we do not have to believe his bravado. It must have been terrifying. At the same time, partly to master it and partly because it was the only emotional contact he had with his father, Mike began playing provocateur.

Mike came to replay the accelerating tempo of his father's fury over and over. The meaning—the frustrated love, the fearfulness, the humiliation—are now mostly suppressed. These ideas resurface in fragments. Mike mentions the street fight with his old partner, starting, significantly, with the line "I always loved humiliating you." Mike tried to walk away, he said, but somehow he couldn't. He also mentions the "panic" of the sale. He was not panicked, of course. It was his customers, somewhat like his mother, who found the mounting excitement frightening.

Now we can see that the sale followed the larger pattern by which playful emotional battling accelerates into more earnest and fearful struggle. Green's, as I mentioned, was to have been Mike's retirement from the fast lane. It was more than a business, it was the incarnation of Mike's expressive personality. He and his staff lavish their personal attention on each customer. Mike likes to describe his staff as a warm, squabbling family. Surely, Mike explains, the attention and ambiance are worth more than the few dollars someone can save at Sears. When Niles citizens prefer economy, Mike feels personally affronted.

Six months before the Dutch auction, Mike put together what he called his First Annual Horse's Ass Sale. A large newspaper ad proclaimed, "Tired of feeling like [here appeared a picture of a horse's hind quarters]? Well, we are." The ad went on to inform readers that Green's offered unusual value, and that it was high time they made the store's acquaintance. "That ad said three things. One, that we are a little bit angry, we are going to semi-insult you if we have to, and we are just going to have a hell of a lot of fun. . . . We are going to gently but directly hit them in the teeth, and kind of defy them to come down and see us."

That first sale began the struggle, cast in Mike's usual playful, embattled style. Six months later it ended in a crescendo of destruction. At the end Mike felt compelled to continue, because there was no line of face-saving retreat.

The essential point, finally, is that all of this reconstructed meaning is lost to Mike. He sees himself as an emotional, warm-hearted man. The misfortunes in his life seem visited upon him by events. I doubt that he even recognizes the repetitive scenario. Yet, as the drum beat quickens, Mike finds himself caught up in an act whose only images are those of movement itself. Then there is panic in the room, and a blind insistence to carry everything to its cataclysmic end. The designified imagery of momentum protects him from the full force of his memories at the cost of enslaving him in compulsive repetition.

Like Ken and Al, Mike describes a father who coupled emotional distance with outbursts of terrifying anger. Like them, Mike denies how frightened he was as a child (though the evidence is not hard to gather) and insists upon how aggressive he has become as an adult. Finally, again like Ken and Al, Mike tells us how much he enjoys the social give-and-take of work. Where Ken is the "coach" and Al is a "counselor," Mike's store is a "family." He is, of course, no more successful than the other two. First of all, what Mike expects from his customers—that they will pay higher prices for family ambience—is unrealistic. Second (and here he resembles Ken and Al once more), Mike cannot really be affectionate with anyone very long. He turns every close encounter into a wrestling match.

The home that Mike describes sounds more frightening than either Ken's or Al's. Their fathers verged on emotional abuse; Mike describes continued, unpredictable violence. Perhaps for that reason, Mike seems to bear the psychological scars of his past more visibly. Like Al, Mike uses career advancement as a way to restore his stature. Mike is more extreme than Al. Although Al has changed course several times, he has also managed to hold a position within a firm for several years and build his position within it. In contrast, Mike seems to have jumped from one company to another, occasionally streaking to stardom, often overreaching himself and falling on his face. But this difference between the two men is essentially one of degree.

More ominously, Mike seems to use the imagery of career movement to reenact the accelerating excitement and violence of his father's anger. Why he should want to replay this scene—an attempt at mastery, an attempt to reevoke the only emotional contact he knew as a child—is a question that only much more extensive exploration could answer.

One way to compare the three men is to ask, "How well does each of them turn the culture of careerism to his psychological defense?" Each man deals with the dilemma of wanting and fearing intimacy at work. Ken uses the idea of acting in role to strike a tense balance between friendship and privacy. Al repeatedly hopes for too much affection, and then uses trajectory to restore his self-esteem. But Mike brings the danger of intimacy—violent assault—into his experience of trajectory itself.

In each of the preceding cases we have seen how psychodynamic needs and careerism make use of each other. I have concentrated largely on one side of this alliance, trying to show how the idea of acting in role or pursuing a career's upward curve sustains psychodynamic defense. But the opposite point is also true. Don and Ken are better managers to the degree that they retain their dispassion; Al is a better salesman because he can pour into his work his "massive energy." In fact, it is more accurate to say that we have seen the profit careerism derives from its alliance with psyche than the other way around. There is a great deal of personal strain in the positions Don and Ken hold, and a cycle of hope, disappointment and counterattack in Al's, but in each case we have at least seen how the man's career is furthered, even if he is not at peace.

Mike is the first example of someone whose career is partly undone by its psychological burden. One way to explain this is to say that Mike is more disturbed than the others. But although this seems to be true, it is an explanation cast in psychological terms. It does not describe his problem in terms of work itself. From a different angle, we might see it this way: although Mike pursues career trajectory, he has fastened upon one corner of it. He does care about getting ahead, of course, but he also has a peculiar fascination with what we have called "acceleration" and "momentum." These are features of career movement, but not the central ones, not the ones that are values of a work ethic. It is as if Mike has seized one corner of the table, and so toppled it over upon himself.

Mike is not alone in his concentration upon side features of trajectory. Lew, whom we will discuss in chapter 11, has a different preoccupation. Lew values moving up, but even more, moving on. The fit between psychodynamic preoccupation and cultural formula is always imprecise. What we make of the social Rorschach, and what it makes of us, is open to negotiation.

8

An Unambitious Man

Ben Goldman, age thirty-six, is associate professor of sociology at Oberlin College. He was granted tenure last year, after having been denied it two years earlier at Williams College. The last three years have been a time of intense anxiety, frustration and finally vindication. Yet now that the struggle is over, the future secure, Ben finds himself questioning his own motivation. Teaching seems more and more an irritation. A small community theater is now the focus of his inspiration. If Ben is younger chronologically than most of the men in this study, the concerns of his life are similar. The tenure system has brought him, earlier than might another career, to a point of self-assessment. Now that he has arrived, he must try to remember where he was going.

Here it is necessary to say some things, if only to get them out of the way. Ben is gay. He did not say so immediately, but the hints and, I gathered, the invitation for me to ask, were there from the first interview. I, feeling probably more circumspect than he, did not ask directly until our third meeting. The question hung between us then for some time, and may have contributed to the atmosphere of friendly but edgy circumspection. I say "might" because I am not at all convinced that the sexual issue was the only, or even the main, cause of that odd atmosphere.

The mood was always lively, engaging, personal. Ben has that self-reflective disposition, which is perhaps what leads some people to pursue academic careers or perhaps is simply what the profession takes as good behavior. I do not know that he is more insightful than other men; however, he was willing to follow my questions wherever they might lead. Surprisingly often his assessment of himself was harshly deprecating.

For all Ben's openness I often felt that we were treading lightly on mined ground. There is an edginess to him that the soft-spoken manner does not disguise. Immediately after the sexual issues were acknowledged, our conversation became more relaxed. It seemed that the personal distance between us diminished. At the same time, what he actually said turned increasingly toward bitterly vengeful imagery, directed alternately at himself and his students. If acknowledging his homosexuality was the license to speak more freely, it seemed to me that the more fragile balance lay between his geniality and his bitterness. In what I have to say here, I will concentrate on the rage that curls around the edges of his soft-spoken friendliness.

In the last two cases I have tried to show how the rising trajectory of career advancement becomes a substitute and disguise for other, suppressed motives. In particular, trajectory offers an aggressive compensation for rejected affection. Ben describes himself as having inverted the usual careerist solution. He says he is no longer interested in advancement. Instead, the chief enthusiasm of his life comes from genuine personal engagement with his students or fellow actors.

We will see that his experience is considerably more complex than this first description allows. Ben has by no means escaped the approved ambitiousness of career culture. His self-proclaimed contentedness is purchased at the price of self-respect. He is as much a prisoner of careerism as those who accept it uncritically. Still, Ben is unusual in that the solution offered by ambition is more apparently conflictual for him than for other men. If he is unable to commit himself to ambitious achievement he is equally unable to surrender it, a point which his own self-contempt only makes more obvious.

Of course we may ask how much of a solution trajectory really offers anyone. Mike was led to ruin; Al now finds himself at sea, assessing his next move. Still, Al and Mike were both able to throw themselves into career advancement even if it did not solve their predicaments. Ben is more internally torn than either of them, and for that reason he cannot allow himself even the imperfect relief they have found in ambition. In understanding the reasons for his inhibition, we will see more clearly what kind of solution trajectory promises.

Ben begins by describing his sense of having reached a plateau in his career. Now that the struggle for tenure is over, he is aware of just how tired he is of teaching. "I have been teaching for twelve years; it is not exciting. I have heard every student comment seventeen times, read the same papers, heard the same excuses. Even when I teach a new course, like this fall, I am viewing it as a pain, and not really enjoying it. . . . I am never nervous, but also I am never thrilled."

What he says is by no means unbelievable. How many times can anyone teach the same material before it wears thin? Yet before we agree too quickly with Ben's description we should know that boredom is a familiar acquaintance in his life. When he was teaching at Williams the student newspaper quoted him as saying, with satisfaction, that he felt married to his job. Yet his name on campus was Ben "I'd-rather-be-anywhere-but-here" Goldman. Each weekend was an opportunity to escape. These days acting is a relief from the classroom, yet it too gets boring. Midway through each play Ben finds himself looking forward to the next, or even thinking more fondly of teaching.

As Ben sees it, he grows bored when the genuineness of human interaction turns into an overrehearsed act. Teaching, for example: "When it is not working is when I remember, 'Oh, this is where I told that funny bit.' That is when I am not enjoying the whole process." It will become clear that, with Ben, boredom is a codeword for a more specific kind of ungenuineness. "Bored" is the way Ben feels when he masks his bitterness behind artificial friendliness.

Several times Ben mentioned how content he is with the direction his life has taken. At the end of our first interview he said, "Thinking about all this makes me even more pleased with the way life is now. I enjoy almost every day." These protestations quickly became unbelievable. In other passages Ben described his professed complacency with cruel mockery.

> At [my undergraduate college] I wanted to get in not the best frat, but the next one down. In high school I was in the second clique, and that is where I decided I belonged. . . . I always thought of myself as a Beta: solid second level...like in *Brave New World*. I am quite content, not driven, not disappointed. . . . I have tendencies toward laziness, and I am satisfied with it. . . . My hero is Bobby Kennedy, because he was exactly the opposite. He would tackle the biggest, toughest thing: Jimmy Hoffa, the Presidency, going for the top. I have never done that.
>
> Everyone at [college] was good-looking, upper-middle-class, popular, leaders—all-around successful, boring people. Almost everyone could have gone to a more famous academic school, and all went [where they did] instead to have a good time and not kill themselves. A good, second-level school.

These passages make clear the contempt Ben has for complacency: his own or what he imagines in his college classmates. He has not renounced ambition, he is consumed by it. Perhaps more exactly, he is obsessed with the dilemma of ambition. Unlike Mike or Al, Ben has been unable to fling himself headlong into career advancement. He cannot take part, but neither can he turn his back and walk away.

We can now begin to lay out the broad frame of the dilemma with which Ben torments himself. Here we will be guided partly by his own terms, partly by the larger interests of this study. First, there is the question of ambitiousness. Is he the good Beta he proclaims himself to be, or is he driven to achieve? This, at least, is the form of the question as Ben asks it. We are not bound to follow his merciless self-interrogation. Ultimately we will ask why he must pose the choice in these insoluable extremes. Second, Ben questions the quality of his relationships with people in his work world, including his students, his old supervisors and his fellow actors.

Cutting across these concerns are two large options for a solution. One side Ben pictures as soft, "nice," personal—and contemptible. The other possibility is tough and impersonal. There is, however, a third possibility, of which Ben is only dimly aware. This choice we may label Cruelty. As I understand him, Ben cannot accept the usual solution of impersonal detachment and ambition because of their association with cruelty. Therefore, he is forced back into a position for which he has little respect: bored, disingenuously friendly mediocrity.

The first choice Ben describes is between teaching and research. Originally he was hired at Williams for his teaching ability. One year before his tenure review he was informed that his publication record was insufficient. He attempted to catch up, failed, and was denied tenure. Now he is at Oberlin, a school that values teaching more than publishing. Yet Ben remains skeptical. "People come to Oberlin not because they are committed to research. Hopefully they are committed to teaching, but sometimes that means nothing; just committed to being lazy. That worries me, that potential in me, that I might treat my job as a part-time thing that I do to get paid." With these lines the main distinction is drawn. Ben likes teaching and, as we will hear, his teaching style is unusually personal. Yet he is skeptical of his preference; teaching, and the student contact it allows, can be an excuse for mediocrity.

While he was still a graduate student Ben had a choice of two advisors. One was a warm, friendly woman; the other, with whom he chose to do his dissertation, was a stern, emotionally abstemious taskmaster. When his father died Ben flew home for the funeral. He returned to a chilly reception from his supervisor: "She made a perfunctory comment: 'I am sorry about your father but you know you have to get back to work.' I staggered across the hall to the other woman I worked for; she put me back together. I came close to switching advisors . . . but something wouldn't allow me to change. I wanted the best. That relates to what I was saying about teaching: I want the hard stuff, not soft."

Ironically, the warmer woman has actually published more, and thereby achieved more of a reputation than the taskmaster, who has hobbled herself by endlessly reanalyzing her data. Ben, however, thinks that the warmer woman has been careless in her research, and that his advisor's style is the more honest academic life. He admires her more than other professors he has known who have achieved national reputations on flimsy research.

The distinction he draws between these two women involves both their professional competence and their friendliness. One is affectionate but perhaps mediocre; the other is punishingly impersonal but dedicated. What is especially interesting about this comparison is the way Ben seems to ignore a plausible alternative construction. In the eyes of the world, the kindly advisor is also the more productive. It is Ben who introduces the stipulation that career dedication of the right kind be stoically impersonal. The wrong kind is practiced by people who are interested in others, who are affectionate, and who become famous. Serious scholarship is harsh and lonely. In this way Ben discounts what might otherwise be the comforting evidence that affiliation and serious professionalism are compatible.

Ben's teaching style is personal and engaging, calculated to break down the distance between himself and his class. In one class on prejudice, he tells an anecdote about how once, in a Spanish hotel, he became convinced he felt bedbugs crawling over him. The point of the story is to show how ready even a staunch liberal like himself is to assume the worst in an alien culture. Ben points out that in telling such a personal story he also erases the distance between himself and his students. The class he most enjoys teaching is the fieldwork seminar. Here he can walk from one small group to another, engaging each student in a more intense demonstration of listening skills.

Ben says that in the last few years he has grown bored with his personal teaching style. The problem is that it has become just an act; it is no longer a way of making genuine contact. Yet we wonder if this is the problem. Looked at more closely, the particular examples just mentioned suggest a more specific dissatisfaction.

The anecdote of the Spanish hotel is more than personal; it is slightly demeaning. Similarly, his teaching style often verges on making himself the butt of a joke. He says, "My style of humor is to be self-deprecatory and a clown. . . . What I do is what I do not like to watch. Slapstick, almost." In a later interview he explained: "I do a Marx brother's walk, which I hate as humor. It offends me; I never laugh. I wouldn't allow myself to laugh. I particularly hate it when it has anything to do with violence. It bothers me when anyone falls down and people laugh. I don't find it funny, and if I did I wouldn't like finding it funny. I wouldn't like myself."

Though Ben says that his humor is never quite slapstick, it heads in that direction. In one class he mimes a famous experiment in which a large, inflatable doll is the victim of a child's aggression. Ben acts out the doll's part.

It begins to sound as if Ben's explanation for his boredom is imprecise. He says that what he misses is the feeling of genuine, spontaneous engagement. We notice that each of his examples of being personal present him in a somewhat demeaning light. Could it be that what he resents is feeling like the inflatable doll: a funny, passive victim? This possibility gains credence when we hear Ben say that his greatest pleasure this year was helping one student learn to express her anger.

Sometimes Ben thinks about how he might change his courses to make them more interesting to both his students and himself. His first idea is to make them more personal. Yet even as he describes this possibility a different note enters his thoughts.

> Another way [to make things better] would be to make my course more like the fieldwork seminar. Take my Sociology of Contemporary Culture course. How does one use that? For our own personal development? For raising children? It intrigues me, but that is exactly what I argued against. Sociology of Contemporary Culture is a garbage course, taught as common sense, not hard-nosed data. It's overly experiential. It is difficult having students talking about their own experience and also cognitive. Without the cognitive part it is not worth it.

Experiential learning falls on the same side of the ledger as his personal but self-deprecating teaching style. The other side is hard-nosed science. Pushing the distinction to its limit, Ben once commented that he has very little interest left in the substance of sociology at all. The only course he still enjoys teaching is research methods. Even in research there are no particular substantive problems that capture his interest. Any research project could be interesting for a while; none is really engaging—at least none that would pass muster with an ethics committee. Here, referring to an earlier conversation we had about Hitler, he explained:

> It all seems irrelevant to me. I don't think sociologists have learned very much. But I think they have a very important perspective: the study of social influence on individuals. What I like in sociology is philosophy and not science, because we are studying something that at least ethically we cannot study scientifically. Very remotely it is connected to Hitler. I was always fascinated with his human experiments, since he could do the sort of experiments that social scientists in their heart of hearts would like to do. I mean I would really like to take a hundred little boys and see if I could make fifty of them turn out homosexual.

Ben's casual reference to the infamous Nazi medical experiments comes as a shock, but perhaps we are overreacting to a chance phrase. We become somewhat more suspicious when we learn that Ben's mother, but not his father, is Jewish. His mother, in fact, was blackballed from a sorority for being Jewish, and quit school. Ben himself felt he was "passing" in college by associating only with non-Jewish friends.

When Ben was six he was taken to a psychiatrist. He is not sure of the reason, except that he was not getting along at all with his father. There were only two visits, because Ben strongly disliked the therapist. "The strongest thing I remember is that he lived in a big scary house, and he looked like Hitler.... I have always remembered it that way, and recounted it that way."

References to Hitler and the Nazis recur often enough in Ben's account to make us wonder what they mean to him. I expect that Jewish identity is only a convenient symbol for summing up many different ways that Ben feels inadequate. He says, "They could all be summarized in the word 'inferior': gay, Jewish, small, and, though I don't really believe it, stupid."

In turn, Ben's fantasy of conducting Nazi-style experiments would allow him to reverse the iniquity, to do unto others as they have done unto him. Ben's description of his childhood psychiatrist continues in this way: "The word 'greasy' comes to mind. . . . The personality I associate with it is sneaky, cruel, might hurt me, can't be trusted, a weasel. . . . Evil, more like Mordred, in fact, and that is how I was made out to look."

The last comment is a reference to a play Ben described in our first interview, in which he had the part of Mordred, the sneaky villain in the legend of King Arthur who sets Arthur and Lancelot at each other's throats and so destroys Camelot. When he first mentioned acting in the play, Ben said he enjoyed it immensely. "I loved being able to be nasty, selfish, blatantly, outrageously cruel and nasty, greedy."

Ben remembers his psychiatrist as a cruel, dangerous man. Yet we cannot help noticing that Ben compares the psychiatrist to roles he himself has played, if only in fantasy. If Ben has played Mordred with glee, if he fantasizes about conducting Nazi medical experiments, then who is victim and who is brutalizer?

As for Ben's fantasies of turning the tables, when he was an undergraduate he actually did conduct one experiment which, if not up to Mengele's standards, was ruled unethical by a college advisory council. The experiment was designed to make students feel helpless. Subjects listened to a droning tone which they were told would cease if they pressed the correct sequence of buttons. In fact, the tone could not be turned off no matter what they did. Among other objections, the council ruled that the tone was too loud. "No one complained, but they said it could be harmful to the ear. I always felt that it was minimally aversive. I wanted it to be louder, because I didn't find it unpleasant. It was boring, perhaps, but not unpleasant. It wouldn't make me do anything."

With this passage we complete a small circle. Earlier, the word "boring" played a prominent part in Ben's description of his life. He is bored with his career, his unambitious mediocrity, his performance as the friendly, enthusiastic teacher. At that point we speculated that behind boredom lay his sense of being too personal, demeaned, and insufficiently aggresssive. Now the word appears again. This time, the opposite of a boring noise would be one that causes real pain.

It bears noticing that Ben's would-be victims look disturbingly like himself. In the Nazi fantasy he would make fifty little boys gay. In the experiment with the loud noise, he was trying to make his subjects feel helpless, perhaps the way he—a small, "inferior" boy—once felt himself.

Ben divides the traits we have heard so far—sociable, nice, perhaps mediocre, and Jewish on one side, cruel, ambitious and solitary on the other—neatly between his parents. His mother is his representative of pure gentleness and, what is significantly related, unambitiousness. His father stands for harsh, driven ambition.

> I saw them as black and white, good and bad, with my father bad and my mother snow-white. I always thought she was the best possible mother, and I still do. I think she is a remarkable woman in a completely unremarkable way. That ties into being boring, too steady, unspectacular, and somewhat dishonest. She is all of that too. . . . She is dishonest with her friends. Nobody has a bad word about her. She is extremely well liked."

In a different passage he said:

> She was always popular, moderately attractive and intelligent. A good solid Beta, or a little lower. I have slightly higher aspirations than her. . . . Her whole goal in life is to make things nice. It bothered her that her husband and son had such a terrible relationship. My father was very much driven all of the time. She has very little drive, and I am a cross.

At times Ben describes himself as being like his mother. He says, for example, "My whole goal in life is to be nice." Yet it is clear, if only from the mocking exaggeration of this line, that he does not really intend us to believe it. He pictures himself as both more assertive and more ambitious than his mother. Still, if he does not see himself as being quite as pure as she, he does tell a set of stories intended as evidence of his distaste for violence. In this line he says that he does not pick flowers; if he sees an ant in the house he will carry it outside rather than kill it. The year between college and graduate school, when he taught fifth grade, he was disturbed by the aggressiveness of his young pupils. Finally, there are two memories from childhood, recounted to illustrate his distaste for violence.

> As a kid I was afraid of violence. . . . I ran from it all the time. I punched a kid in kindergarten, he got a bloody nose and I was terrified. I haven't been in a fight since. I hated snowball fights; I would walk two miles to avoid one. Once they were all throwing snowballs at a window. I wouldn't, and they teased me, so I took a big clod of snow and of course I broke the window. I was just terrified. . . . It ties to my feeling [of being] small and vulnerable. . . . That is why all my friends were female, not threatening. I had a few male friends, who I could dominate by the force of my will.

Ben recounts these stories as evidence that he was an unusually fearful child. He may well have been, yet these stories suggest something beside his fear. They also tell us what he imagines may be true about his own potential for violence. Ben is the one who broke the window and bloodied the other child's nose. When he spoke of slapstick earlier, the most revealing line may have been, "I would not like to like it." Only someone unusually concerned about his own destructiveness would make a point of mercy with insects and flowers.

This cluster of images is slightly more pacific than Ben usually pictures himself. More often, with his customary cynicism, he describes himself as covertly aggressive.

> Did I ever tell you that my favorite sport is football? Defensive lineman. I like to rush the passer. It is interesting, because the words I use to describe myself in that position are sneaky, quick, elusive....
>
> There is a part of me that is very Machiavellian. And that part probably runs at odds with the part of me that wants to be brave, honest and direct. I want to be the guy behind the scenes having control that no one knows. On the other hand, I want to be very sincere, genuine, above-board, and not have to play games.

If Ben pictures himself as a gentle soul (though covertly aggressive), he describes the men in his family, reaching back five generations, as epitomes of cruel, self-centered machismo. Ben's great-great-grandfather was an enormously wealthy man, a member of that peerage of nineteenth-century financiers now fondly called the Robber Barons. His grandfather was a swashbuckler in his own right. After leaving his wife and children, he lived the glamorous life in Europe. He was a war correspondent who stayed on in Paris; for a time he gadded about with Hemingway and Fitzgerald. Ben, who knew him only as an old man, speaks of him now with a mixture of affection, admiration, bitterness and attempted derision. "He thought he was terrific and really wasn't much . . . He was terrific by association: a wealthy family, he knew Fitzgerald and Hemingway, had a way with women. . . . He was intriguing, smart, good sense of humor, well read. He has written a few pieces that are reasonably well written—boring but literate. He wrote better than I do."

One piece of this story is especially interesting simply because Ben finds it significant enough to remember. At one point a business venture of his grandfather's fell into financial straits. He turned to his wealthy family for support, but ran into difficulties. His mother, rather than his father, was the heir to the fortune. However, since only the male children controlled the fortune, the grandfather was forced to plead his suit to his uncles instead of his mother.

This is the first example of a family history whose title might be "Inadequate Sons and Emasculated Fathers." As Ben understands it, his father felt driven to achieve a success commensurate with his famous family. Ben believes that his father always felt like a failure. As for Ben, he recalls his grandfather saying to an acquaintance, "I never thought any of my grandchildren were especially attractive." With the story of the grandfather's failing business, both Ben's humiliation and his father's are reversed. The grandfather is made a supplicant for a favor from his powerful family. As the story concludes, only token assistance was ever provided, and the grandfather "was very bitter about that."

The story of Ben's father follows exactly the same plot. He too was a big man, a wrestler and football player at the University of Chicago. With his characteristic mixture of admiration and derision Ben says, "He was a benchwarmer back when the University of Chicago was in the Big Ten." (Here we might recall that Ben's favorite sport is to sack the quarterback.) As Ben describes it, the father's career was a failure. A wealthy college friend employed him as a roving trouble-shooter. "My father became basically his slave. He worked for years for this man, long hours, low wages, always being called off in the middle of the night. My mother was miserable. She never saw him. He worked incredibly hard, and didn't seem to get much for it."

Whether Ben's father saw himself in this light is something we can never tell. As a story, it repeats the theme of the grandfather. The tyrant of Ben's youth gets his comeuppance, if not directly at the hands of his son then indirectly. If Ben is inadequate, his father is more so.

We come finally to Ben himself. Here, the heart of his recollection is how much a disappointment to his father he felt himself to be.

> I was a continual disappointment to him. He wanted me to be everything: captain of the football team, president of the class, straight A's, and more than that he wanted me to be very self-confident, which of course I wasn't at all. . . . I was very sensitive, got my feelings hurt, was a disgrace as a boy because I cried in public. . . .
>
> I felt inferior, unattractive, unpopular, very small. In high school I had skin problems. I always felt a freak.
>
> I was afraid of [my father] in every way. . . . There were a couple of times when he would lash out at me physically. He had a temper and would just swing at me or try to kick me in a very uncontrolled way. I was never seriously hurt. But the idea. . . . I was crushed, devastated by it. There was no underlying relationship, no trust, no feeling of love. I didn't even like him.

When Ben thinks of his father now, it is mostly with sadness and even, he says, with forgiveness. "I learned to like him once I left home. He was really a neat guy, very funny, caring, sensitive. He just didn't know how to be involved. He had no parents when he was growing up and he just did not know what to do."

In this passage Ben sounds like Mike, who also forgives a father who was violent, demeaning, and emotionally unapproachable. Mike's reconciliation, you may recall, was something less than perfect. Mike has a disturbing habit of reenacting a scenario in which affection escalates into violence. It turns out that Ben's forgiveness also leaves room for doubt. Speaking here of the faculty who denied him tenure, all older men, not as qualified or productive as the younger faculty (could he have in mind another older man?), he says:

> Understanding prevents me from being really angry at anyone in the world.... I think about Hitler, and I am sorry about what he did.... My behavioristic orientation makes me think, "Given these events, you were fated to do that." My good friend believes that someone is always to blame. I think it is just the situation, or an accident, or just being insensitive to each other's needs. No disgrace.

As we know, Ben usually invokes Hitler in connection with his most vengeful fantasies. If he forgives his father as he forgives Hitler, we suspect just how furiously unpardoning he really feels.

In describing his relationship with his father Ben sounds remarkably like Ken, Al or Mike. All of them describe fathers who were emotionally erratic, at times violent, other times distant, rarely capable of affection, who made them feel frightened and demeaned. Each of these men attempts to establish personal bonds with people in their work world: with a protégé, a boss, customers. Ben tries to establish this sort of intimacy with his students. All of them eventually fail, and feel humiliated for having made the effort. Ken, Al and Mike save their pride with furious ambition. Ben, however, calls himself a "contented Beta." What is the difference?

A reasonable answer must acknowledge several things. First of all, we should not take Ben's self-description too literally. He certainly is not content, and he does not really want anyone to believe that he is merely mediocre. But it is true that he is not as overtly, joyously aggressive in his pursuit of career advancement as the others.

Some of the reason may have to do with his self-confidence, going back to things as basic as what growing boys believe about their bodies. Ken was an athlete, Mike was a hellion. Ben was a small boy who, especially compared with his father's example and expectation, felt physically inadequate. Ben may have given up on overt aggression a long time ago. He himself says something like this. His explanation, given with his usual mocking candor, is that he is afraid to try. Suppose he tried for an A and failed? Settling for B's is so much safer.

Perhaps this is the answer. Ben may have accepted so much of what he believed to be his father's disdain that he is afraid to try. I would argue for a different understanding. His less conscious fear is that the only victory that would make up for his injury would be uncontainably vengeful. This thought is too frightening, and so Ben practices a denial in two parts. He pretends to a phony gentleness that even he knows is not genuine, and he agrees with his father's presumed judgment of his mediocrity.

Like Ken, Al, or Mike, Ben attempts to create personal relationships at work that will make up for the affection he missed as a child. But these attempts are never satisfying. Like the other men from whom we have heard, Ben's experience of current relationships is always infiltrated by old memories of humiliation. He himself brings this to pass by describing his squeamishness over imaginary bedbugs and miming the part of a beaten doll. Having turned his attempted moment of closeness into something demeaning, Ben then reacts punitively. He imagines turning half his students gay, or making them feel helpless. That is, he imagines subjecting them to the ways he feels inferior. The problem, however, is that Ben's fantasies of turning the tables feel to him as if they might get out of control. When he finally responds to provocation and fights back, he bloodies a schoolmate's nose or breaks a window. Ben would very much like to humiliate his tormentors, much as the stories he tells of his family emasculate several generations of male forebears. He is unable to try, partly because he fears he will be unsuccessful but partly because he fears becoming uncontrollably destructive. (The logic of the unconscious, which tolerates the simultaneous presence of thoughts that are consciously irreconcilable, make it possible for Ben to be plagued by both anxieties.)

Ben's problem may be summarized in his most descriptive word: every new project in which he invests himself soon grows "boring." Although he says he grows bored when he can no longer be personal, we now see the matter in a different light. He grows bored when he is disingenuously nice and mediocre (he suspects that seemingly nice people like his mother and himself are not completely honest) and when he is not aggressive. The word "boring" also shows us why he cannot be aggressive. In order for the droning noise in his college experiment to have stopped being boring it would have had to have been painful. The choices Ben sees are between being nice and mediocre or ambitious and cruel. His own capacity for cruelty worries him too much for that road to be a solution.

In placing Ben's case within the larger context of this study, we may note several things. First, although Ben does not avail himself of the imperfect solution ambition offers, the logic of his situation is no different from that of the other men. We can understand his position by referring it to the same main coordinates that made other cases intelligible: the cultural problem of collegiality and dispassion, the imperative of ambition, and the psychodynamic problem of affection, humiliation, and aggressive self-defense.

Second, although Ben cannot make use of the solution career trajectory offers, he cannot escape it either. He tries. He tells us that after some initial setbacks and much hard work he has achieved job security. He has friends in town, an on-going relationship, and interesting activities outside of work. By most standards it seems an enviable catalogue. But Ben cannot stop there. He must continue, and explain that in terms of ambition he is really content to be mediocre. The imperative of career trajectory confronts him. If it cannot be his solution, it is now an accusation. His situation is the exact reciprocal of that in which women who pursue careers find themselves. As women often say, no matter how successful they are in their work the question "Yes, but what has she done about her family?" always hangs in the background. The same question, these women correctly point out, is not leveled at an ambitious man. Ben, at this point, finds himself domestically secure. But neither the culture, nor he himself, is going to let him rest easy. He compares himself to his mediocre, comfort-seeking mother. Though he mocks them, he knows that none of the men in his family—nor the ghost of Hemingway—would approve.

The final point this case suggests departs from the history Ben tells of his family. Unable to defeat his family by his own activity, for whatever combination of self-doubt and inhibition, Ben diminishes them by the story he tells of their careers. This is not the usual sense in which we think of careers solving the problem of internalized parental relationships. But it is a common enough strategy, one that also operates within the rhetorical and theatrical opportunities provided by career culture. This is where we turn next.

Part Four

Stories Men Tell

9

Family Legends

In each of the cases I have presented so far I have tried to show how men use their careers to transform an internalized relationship with their parents. It would be going too far to say that these are solutions. The first two men, Don and Ken, end up preserving a tense balance. Their success is limited to persuading themselves that their own agitation or vulnerability will not interfere with their work. The next group of men all use career trajectory as a vehicle of aggression, to restore their diminished sense of self. Their success is also highly equivocal. Al, and even more so Mike, find themselves locked in repetitive cycles of hope, disappointment, and counterattack. Ben, who finds a similar meaning in trajectory but cannot avail himself of the opportunity it offers, feels mediocre and bored. Although their solutions are painfully limited, we have the sense with all of them, except perhaps Ben, that the resolutions they reach allow them some psychic relief, and also allow them to drive their careers forward.

There is an alternative possibility, which is actually foreshadowed by Ben's case. Rather than using a career to change oneself, one can use it to change the internal representation of a parent. In some measure, of course, this always happens. As Schafer (1968) points out, any representation of "self" is implicitly a representation of self-in-relation-to-another. If a career changes one, it also, inevitably, changes the other. But this is a more-and-less affair. The men from whom we have heard so far (Ben excepted) use their careers primarily to alter, in adult scenarios, the child they once were. The next two men, Bob and Lew, use their careers primarily to alter their image of their fathers.

How is this possible? Obviously one cannot change another person, much less change who that person was some time ago. But one can change a memory or a history. One can remember details selectively, or choose to emphasize one construction of events over another. That is what these men do. Bob describes his father's career in terms that make him seem less ambitious than he really was, while Lew remains loyal to a myth of his father's early life that makes him seem more adventurous.

It is a difficult matter to compare Bob and Lew with the other informants. For instance, it would be inaccurate to say that they are less well adjusted. Of the men in this study, Mike is probably the one who has most trouble conducting his life. Compared to him, Bob and Lew are models of stability. Nor would it be right to say that in Bob's or Lew's case we have more self-deception. The problem, more exactly, is that we sometimes feel Bob and Lew are so involved reinventing their father's careers that they never quite get around to caring about their own.

Bob, for example, has wanted to retire since he was in his mid-thirties. Lew is more complicated. He is an immensely energetic man who delights in telling people about the adventurousness of his life. Yet at times his guard slips and we see his doubt. Lew says that he likes living on the cream, the glittery surface, but he wonders if there is any substance to his life. At one point he described listening to several friends talk about their jobs. It all seemed so boring. And then suddenly he found himself thinking, "Why isn't there anything like this in my life, that I care enough about to drone on and on over?"

The stories that these two men tell and, in Lew's case, perform, use the same images and behavior with which we are now familiar. From a different angle, then, they show us the uses of career as a kind of theater in which the internal dialogue of fathers and sons is reenacted and very imperfectly altered.

10

Why the Uncle Died

The most important thing to be said about Bob's career is that it is not really his own. Bob, who is now forty-one, is the manager of a small manufacturing company started by his father and uncle forty years ago. For his father it was a Horatio Alger story come true: out of Detroit's Polish ghetto to the west side suburbs, an illegal attic machine shop grown to a $3-million-a-year business. But this is the father's story; Bob has not risen anywhere. He entered the family business indifferently, when his father's patience and financial support finally ran out on Bob's youthful temporizing. If the career task of forty is to become one's own man, Bob finds himself more than ever his father's delegate. He says, "It is a strange relationship. Not many people who are forty-one spend more time with their father than with their wife and family."

Over the last ten years, as his father has grown older, Bob has in fact made the business more his own, taking over responsibility for daily operations. Two years ago the cruelest irony began: the business is now going bankrupt, victim, like so many others, of Michigan's slumping auto economy.

This bankruptcy is our window onto the meaning of the career. Bob's misfortune is our opportunity. The picture we are offered, however, is indistinct. The sheer factual details of finance and bankruptcy legalisms occupy a large part of this account, all the more because a certain factualism is Bob's preferred style of defense. The gist of the case, however, is this: It would be a disaster for Bob to lose the company. He has driven himself mercilessly to hold together the crumbling pieces. Not only his own welfare but his father's creation is at stake, and Bob is acutely aware of his father's pain. And yet, there is a suggestion that Bob exaggerates the importance of the impending bankruptcy to his father. The hints are subtle, but they accumulate. Eventually they suggest an unconscious thought: terrible as it would be, the bankruptcy would also represent freedom, and perhaps revenge.

Bob, of course, would deny this. His denial makes use of the familiar strategies career culture puts at his disposal: the idea of dispassionate, businesslike relationships and the imagery of career trajectory. But here there is a variation. Since Bob has not been able to use his own career to leave his father behind, he does the reverse. Like Lew, he tells a story about his family, a legend whose moral is that the father never really cared about the business all that much after all. This myth defends the father against Bob's fear—or is it wish?—that the bankruptcy will break his heart. It also defends the father against Bob's accusation that he and his business coerced Bob into giving up his youthful freedom.

I must emphasize that Bob is not at all looking forward to the demise of the business. Consciously he is aware only of the impending disaster. If there is another side to the story, it is nothing he would acknowledge. Therefore let us begin with what is clearer and closer to Bob's own experience. The approaching bankruptcy leads Bob into a discussion of loyalty and impartiality in business relations. This portion is worth listening to in itself if only because Bob so neatly illustrates the conflicts and rhetoric of business friendliness. Beyond this, we will begin to hear the accusations Bob unconsciously levels at his father, and the defense he attempts to offer.

At the time of these interviews the company was in a Chapter Eleven bankruptcy. The court had declared a moratorium on payment of all bills. Bob had several months to pull the business back together. The fate of the company was likely to rest on the decisions of a few key outside players—his creditors, who made up his board of overseers, and several large buyers of machine parts, whose purchase orders would tip the balance one way or the other. Their decisions would be based in part on financial considerations, but partly on personal sentiment, loyalty to an old friend and customer, or possibly vindictiveness. Not only was Bob uncertain of the outcome, he was decidedly ambivalent on the whole question of how large a part personal feeling should play.

At one point he suggested that his creditors might force him to liquidate simply out of their own anger, despite the fact that destroying him will in no way benefit them. He has no hidden money to pay them. Somewhat surprised, I asked whether business is really so personal an affair. He replied,

> Business is interpersonal dealings. For twenty-five years my father called the head of the steel company. "Hi Irv, I need 10,000 pounds of so-and-so next week, and have you any so-and-so today." It is like a fruit peddler, for crying out loud. Do you have any five-sixteenths nuts today? Do you have any pears? On our level, we are carrying on no different than they were bartering in Mesopotamia five thousand years ago."

In this passage, the corner grocery image of business sounds affectionate. The remainder of this discussion, however, soon headed off in a very different direction. Bob abhors the personal diplomacy of business. He describes obsequious salesmen who cozy up to the fatuous managers of big car companies, men whose casual decision can mean a million-dollar contract won or lost. He himself is acerbically plainspoken. Here he describes a relationship where there is no illusion of affection on either side.

B: He wouldn't give me the time of day, and I feel the same way. . . . He perceives me as arrogant, looking down on him.

RO: He couldn't be right about that, could he?

B: He is dead nuts on. But that's not a reason to dislike me, because I happen to be able to perceive accurately [*laughing*]. If we are talking business, that shouldn't be sufficient reason for not dealing with someone.

Here I tried to clarify my own confusion. Does Bob think business should be impersonal? He had just finished describing the computerlike approach of General Motors with evident distaste. Was he now saying he preferred machinelike impartiality?

B: You should put it in the computer and kick it out the other way.

RO: You would like it that way?

B: *(pause)* It should be personal in that you can talk to the people you are doing business with. You shouldn't have to knuckle under to them. They shouldn't be using their position to beat you into submission; using their financial power to their own personal advantage. . . . You should be able to talk to a guy and divorce your personal relationship from business. You can't have it both ways; I appreciate that.

Yet it seems that Bob is trying to have it both ways. Business decisions should not be personal, he says. At the same time, all last summer he found himself in heated arguments with his liberal Oak Park friends, who went on buying Toyotas while Detroit fell apart.

You talk to people about Tisch [an amendment to cut property taxes] and they say, "That's terrible; people will be out of jobs." And I say, "Do you know how many people *are* out of jobs? We are in a depression, and you don't feel it. Now it is coming close to you, and you are worried. But two years ago, when I said 'Consider buying an American car,' you didn't do that. You want me to vote for you, against Tisch, but you won't vote for me in the marketplace."

In the largest sense it is true that Bob may be losing his business to the foreign car invasion. Yet even so, his grievance is unusual. How many people would seriously expect their neighbors to alter a decision involving thousands of dollars out of personal loyalty? Bob describes this as a personal affront: "You voted against me." The vast indifference of global economics comes down to neighbor against neighbor.

The question of favoritism arises often enough to suggest that it is a lively issue in Bob's life. On the whole, he prefers to deny its importance. However, these denials are too vehement. In the end we are more convinced that Bob feels cheated than that he is indifferent.

For example: Bob's sister lives in Detroit, in a house bought for her by their father, ostensibly as an investment. At that time, the father gave Bob a gift of equivalent value, in shares of company stock. The original deal called for the sister to provide the monthly mortgage payments. However, the sister and her husband have rarely been able to make their monthly payments, so the "investment" has become, in fact, more of a gift. Now that the company is failing, the father has started to regret his division of the spoils. Bob's sister has a house; Bob has only a quantity of stock in a worthless company. The father would like to correct the imbalance, but Bob refuses to acknowledge the whole issue of favoritism. His very denial, however, makes clear his sense of injustice.

> My father says, "I have two children. One is benefitting, and you are not getting anything." And I say, "I don't give a shit. I'm not looking for anything." It is not mine; it is his to do whatever he chooses [with]. If the estate were divided equally between me and my sister, her share would be mine, and one half the estate. And if that is what he wants to do, or wanted at the time he wrote his will, whether or not he chose ever to consider rectifying that imbalance, it is his business. I am not getting short-changed; I don't feel I am. I think it is stupid the way they are acting toward my sister. I think they are not helping her out at all. I think they are hindering her development.

Bob's last remark about his sister's development has its own significance. When I asked, "Why do your parents become involved this way with your sister and not with you?" he replied, "Because I never stood for it. I took money from them only through my college education." As we will hear, the actual events were rather different than this answer suggests. Bob joined the company when his father stopped supporting him financially. His entry into the company marked the end of his youthful independence, and he resented it. When he says, "I never stood for it," he is rewriting a frustrating episode of his own history.

At the time his father bought the house Bob warned his parents that property values in Detroit were certain to decline. If they wanted to give his sister a house, Bob said, that was fine, but please don't pretend that it is an investment. The maddening upshot of the whole affair was that property values rose. The gift turned out to be an investment after all. Bob concludes, "So now it turns out that he is making a horrendous amount of money on this house." Why "horrendous"?

The father is apparently going to get away with something that Bob never allows himself to attempt. Bob never asks for personal favors (although he would like to). He always couches his request in the impersonal terms of mutual business advantage. For example, Bob sells machine parts to Ford, and it appears that Ford's purchasing agent is considering a change to another supplier. The decision makes some sense from a business point of view: Bob's company may go under at any moment. On the other hand, Bob is an old business associate. There is potential claim on loyalty; however, the actual argument Bob advances is specifically not personal.

> I told him, "I make a high-quality part for you, which means no rejections for you either. Now we are in financial trouble, and the corporate head seems to prefer to give the job to someone else, as opposed to helping me out. If you could speak to him, tell him, 'Here is a quality supplier we don't want to lose,' I will improve my financial situation and be better able to help you in the future." I said, "Help us if you want to. If not, try someone else, and maybe they will be as good, and maybe not."

In giving Bob's sister the house, the father has violated the rule to which Bob holds himself. Bob refuses to ask for personal favors, although he will point out the mutual business advantage to someone who can help him. This is a stern code, and we can imagine that Bob is quite sensitive to anything that smacks of bending the rules. His father seems to have violated the principle. He has given Bob's sister quite a substantial gift—a house—and he is going to get away with pretending that it was an "investment" after all. Bob will not say that he thinks it is unfair, but his word "horrendous" tells us anyway.

Bob's description of his dealings with Ford's purchasing agent points up a different aspect of how he defuses the issue of personal loyalty. He says, "If I go broke, you will lose too." In this way, he removes control of the situation from both his hands and the agent's. The agent does not have to make a personal decision, and Bob does not have to make a personal claim; both of them simply have to observe which way neutral events are forcing them to move.

I might mention a similar situation that arose in the course of the interviews. At one point Bob was anticipating a court hearing that might have forced him out of business. If that happened, he said, "I will no longer be in crisis, and I won't be able to come talk to you any more." I said, "I am not just interested in your crisis." He replied, "Well then, maybe I'll come back." What is this exchange?

Superficially, it is a misunderstanding about the nature of this project. Bob imagines I am doing a study only of midlife crisis, instead of careers in general. Once his crisis is over, he thinks he will no longer be interesting. When the misunderstanding was clarified, he agreed to continue. But is that really what happened here?

Although Bob, like several of the men I interviewed, let me know that he was skeptical of psychotherapy, he also mentioned once or twice that it was a relief to talk to someone. Our partnership, therefore, was ambiguous: he was clearly helping me, but perhaps I was also offering him something. His comment, "I won't be able to come to talk to you anymore," suggests that it would be a loss for him too. His remark reveals an exaggeration of our relationship in opposite directions. It becomes more personal: we are not just doing research, this is also therapy. It also becomes less personal: I don't really care about his life; I only care about his crisis. Finally, he gets us both off the hook: a neutral event—a court hearing—will make the decision for us. This tension about loyalty and disinterest, and its resolution by neutral, uncontrollable events, is exactly like his approach to Ford's purchasing agent.

Bob's description of these events denies not only how personal they actually feel; more particularly, they deny his sense of coercion. In effect he says, "No one is forcing me to do anything; it is just the situation." Yet the idea of coercion arises often enough for us to understand that it is an unresolved dilemma in Bob's life. Recall his remark that no one should "force you to knuckle under . . . or beat you into submission."

The purchasing agent to whom Bob appealed for special consideration is one man who wields tremendous power at this moment. Bob refused to appeal on the basis of friendship, preferring the impersonal rationality of business. There is another feature worth noting. Bob turned the powerlessness of his position to advantage. "Help me or I will go under," he said, "and that will hurt both of us." It is a kind of business jujitsu: Bob renounces all power in the face of overwhelming events, and renders a potential opponent helpless as well.

> I can only present fact, which takes on the appearance of strategy. It is really not a strategy. Business is often not a matter of decisions. The mystique of the big decision makers is largely bullshit. They are mostly yes and no decisions. It is the same with Ford: either help me, or put me out of business. These decisions are simply a matter of fact. . . . It's an old legal thing. There they are, *nolo contendere.* You are looking at it; how do you see it? And you call it.

Is this strategy of the forced move only a response to the special circumstance of going broke? When I pointed out the pattern I saw, Bob said that this was only a strategy of last resort. Yet he seems to describe many situations in analogous terms; not only his own, but requests that other people make of him. Here he describes his wife's reaction to the ordeal of the last months:

> At one point my wife asked, "How long are you going to do this?"
> "How long am I going to do what?"
> "Beat your head against a wall. It is not good for anyone; you are not fun, not friendly."
> I said, "However long it takes."

She said, "Well, if I know it will end at some point we will get through it. If it is going to last forever, I don't want any part of it."

It wasn't a threat or an ultimatum, just a statement of fact. It is not a good way for the kids to live.... That is good. It makes you say, "Oh, I guess it is that bad."

The wife is pictured as speaking calmly. These are the facts, she says, now you call it. The question "How long will this continue?" is worth remembering. As we will hear, Bob's father once asked the same question. The link lies in Bob's understanding. In neither case, he claims, was there any anger, disappointment, or test of wills—only the cool presentation of unarguable facts.

Bob's sensitivity to coercion and favoritism appears in every part of his account. It colors his experience of business, his adult relationship with his father and sister. There are memories in a similar vein all the way back to childhood. He defends himself against acknowledging them through a tactic that by now is familiar to us: the rhetoric of business pragmatism. It is a code that denies all personal motive in favor of indifferent fact. None of this is new; Bob speaks, more insistently than many men, the common language of work.

Now, however, we turn to something that is unusual. Unlike the other cases we have heard so far, Bob has not used his career to escape from family, not even in the superficial, minimally satisfying way of Al, Mike or Ken. His career is, instead, a continuing reminder of family troubles. Bob works side by side with his father. He has never broken free. Now, as the bankruptcy approaches, his real concern mixes with unconscious fantasies of freedom and, perhaps, violently pushing his father off his back.

This portion of the interpretation must rely on more ambiguous evidence. Certainly Bob himself would never agree with this view. We must rely on the accumulated weight of small hints in his account. To begin, there is the history of how he came to join the business.

Bob went to a Catholic prep school and a Jesuit, all-male college. Then he came to Ann Arbor for law school. There are people from the East Coast and California who think of Ann Arbor as a cow town with cultural pretensions. For Bob, "It was like moving from Kansas to New York City." He succumbed to whatever version of bright lights and fast living he found on South University Street, and flunked out of law school. He says, "It was a very traumatic period. It was the first time it was really demonstrated to me that I would not be allowed to stay there, even if I wanted to."

The way he puts it is interesting. Someone else might have said, "It was the end of my plans for a career." Bob says, "I would not be allowed to stay." Permission, and especially permission to pursue his own interests, is the loss Bob experienced. He transferred to business school, "and suddenly the funding ran out. My father figured I was old enough to pay for myself. He asked, could I tell him how long I would be in school? And I said, 'Gee, no.'... And he said he basically didn't think he was willing to foot that tab much longer. So, having run out of funds, I went home."

He went back to Detroit, where he spent the next three years going to business school classes in the evening and teaching high school during the day. "And then you got to go to work, right? I wasn't a whiz; I couldn't go on for a Ph.D. in something. I didn't know what to get a Ph.D. in. So I just went to work. I asked my father if I could do anything. Business was expanding; they actually needed help. So I went to work and that was that."

His very next comment was, "So it's always been there. It would be like a very close friend dying if it wasn't there." Undoubtedly it would. Still, there is room for ambivalence even when close friends die. Bob entered the family business not with any love for metal or machines, nor even money, but simply because time had run out.

While we are at this point, it is worth hearing what Bob had to say about a different sort of premature commitment, a girlfriend from his college days: "We started talking—we, she—about when we were going to be engaged, married. And I had always intended to do things. In high school I wanted to travel, to indulge myself, to be good to myself for a while.... What scared me was projecting a feeling I know I am capable of: in ten years, or five, discovering you had not done those things you promised yourself you would do, and blaming her."

It is the same issue. Youthful freedom is the hope, cheerless adult responsibility the antagonist. Bob is now married, happily, as near I can tell. In that sphere of his life commitment has been worthwhile. His parallel concerns about both career and marriage suggest that at twenty freedom seemed hemmed in on all sides. The father in particular put an end to dalliance, first by cutting off support, then by offering a career that would bind Bob to home. And now, what does the business mean?

> I am forty-one. Four years ago I told some people, "By the time I am forty, I want that place running so it can run without me. So I can pursue whatever interests I have in addition to business, and it won't cry out for my hand...." Which should be the sign of a good anything—a department, a house. It can run without you because people know what to do in your absence. I said either that or I will be out of it.... So I found myself at forty, and now forty-one, clawing to keep the business alive, and seeing it basically slipping through my fingers.

What should we make of this passage? Bob does not say he wanted the business to end; he wanted it to run without his continual presence. Still, it is noteworthy that by his midthirties Bob was already looking forward to detaching himself from his career. Compare him to Ken, who at thirty-seven is planning to double his company's volume in the next year or two. For Bob, this business is not the vehicle of his energy and ambition. It is a weight, a barrier to everything else he would do if only there were time.

It is not difficult to imagine Bob, newly free of Jesuit rectitude, feeling himself too quickly shunted back to responsibility. For this alone he might resent his father and his business. Yet there are other memories, back to childhood, that suggest a similar theme. In these, his father again is an agent of constraint. Here I wish to concentrate on a few brief images Bob offers of his childhood relationship with his father. In general, he says, his father was very busy. He did become involved with the Boy Scouts when Bob joined a troop. Bob suspects that his mother may have encouraged her husband to spend more time with his son.

B: One thing he did do for *me*, specifically, at age eleven I joined the Boy Scouts and he became involved.

RO: What was he like with you?

B: When there were other boys around he took very little shit from me and made sure that if I was doing anything I probably got more than my share of the punishment, simply because he did not want anyone to think he was playing favorites....

Boy Scouts were always good stuff—fishing, hiking. I think I may have felt— I was really not a very good athlete as a kid. There were two things that I was not as good at, that maybe would have pleased him more if I had been better— sports and math.

RO: Do you have any special good memories?

B: Good memories . . . I can remember playing catch with my father, and not being very good at it.... There is a good memory that I have of growing fruit in our backyard. I can so keenly remember the goodness of that.... But that has almost as much to do with my father's father as my father.

Notice in these passages the whole issue of fairness and favoritism. The father's exaggerated fairness contrasts with the suggestion that he really was too busy for his son, that Bob was a disappointment to him, that only the mother's insistence was responsible for even this much contact.

Bob does not say all this, of course. His intention is to recall pleasant memories. Almost without his noticing, however, the "good stuff" turns to doubt. The best memory he can manage turns out to be more about his grandfather than his own father. Coercion is also part of these recollections.

I can remember him whipping me, twice. Both times I think it was for the same offense. One time I was playing. Dinner was at six; I didn't get home until 7:30. It was probably more that my mother was frantic that pissed him off, rather than that I wasn't there. He probably would not have fed me. He took his belt out. Oh, that was the ultimate punishment, not getting hit, but the threat. He would hold his belt out and say, "Smell it." Oh, and you'd hold your breath and say, "I am not going to smell that Goddamn belt." It would be this battle of wills. Shit, he didn't do anything but stand there; you had to breathe sometime.... And the other time these two little girls called me out during dinner, and I stayed out real late, and when I got in all the dishes were put away, and he "wanted to see me."

This last passage is interesting both for what it says and the characteristic denial. In both instances Bob's offense was in prolonging a moment of carefree independence. The father enforces the rule of time. The parallel to Bob's college years is unmistakable.

The denial is also familiar. As Bob recalls, his father did not actually hit him; he was forced to smell the belt. It is the same *nolo contendere* denial that Bob uses now, and ascribes to his wife. There is no arguing with nature, and therefore no reason to impute personal motive to natural inevitability. The conclusion Bob encourages is that his father really did not do anything, and probably did not care one way or the other. The mother might have been angry, the father just stood around holding his belt. The child who held his breath, we may surmise, knew a struggle when he saw one. As an adult, Bob is willing to reconstruct history in passionless colors. This passage is a first example of Bob's denial of his father's willfulness. The second example, also a historical fable, concerns the history of the business. I will return to it soon.

Suppose the business does go under? Bob will be out of a job. He can probably find a managerial post in Detroit. If not, the Sun Belt may offer something. Neither choice delights him. He likes running his own shop; he would prefer not to move. Still, he knows he will not starve.

His father, on the other hand, might take the loss very hard. He is sixty-eight, and the business has been his life. Bob fears that the loss might destroy his father completely. When Bob pictures the final auction his imagination is especially vivid.

I would enter a new phase after foreclosure, and work toward liquidation. Because my father couldn't stand to do it; it would be too traumatic. You stand there and watch the absolute dregs of the earth come in and bid peanuts for stuff he worked years to build up. The guy comes in with the gavel and goes, "How much for that lamp?" And someone goes, "Ach, a nickel." Or some number. And if it is not raised he takes it out for a nickel.

In another discussion he says, "This is my father's mistress we are talking about."

Bob's concern for his father is genuine, and not implausible. Yet, taking into account the history we already know, it might occur to us that his concerns are somewhat exaggerated, and his eye for the humiliation involved unusually keen. As it turns out, the father would not be left destitute by the bankruptcy. He would be left with a $200,000 home, of which all but a small fraction is paid off, and a $300,000 building which is exempt from foreclosure. He might be temporarily cash-poor, but he certainly would not be penniless.

Emotionally, the father seems to have pulled back from the failing business and invested himself in other projects. There is his daughter's house, of which we have already heard. There is also a small paper products company that he began two years ago, which might flourish. Either of these projects could be seen as evidence that the father is not about to retire to twilit old age. Yet somehow Bob finds little encouragement here. He says, "He is withdrawing a little from the reality of what is going on. At the same time, his personal life is more intense than it needs to be." This last line is a deprecating reference to the father's involvement in his daughter's house. As for the paper company, Bob is reluctant to become involved in this project even though the father has encouraged him. "I don't think there is another labor of love left in him. He's done it. I don't think you do that many times in a life. I don't think you do that at sixty-eight. If I could get into a business, a wonderful one in metal, where we could carve a nice little niche for him, I'd dearly love to have him around."

Bob pictures his father as an old man, foolishly involved in projects that are either unsound (the sister's house) or beyond his capacity. He would like to protect his father, safe on some shelf. Yet we gather that the father is not ready for pasture. Why is Bob so quick to see his father's frailty, so skeptical of his new enthusiasms?

It seems to me that there is more to Bob's imagination than simple concern for plausible events. Bob is aware not only of the real threat to his father, but also of the possibility that his father will feel humiliated and broken. It begins to seem possible that Bob's solicitousness defends his father against Bob's own resentment. Of course, as is the nature of defense, his concern betrays the fantasy even in the moment of denial. His description of the auction lingers on his father's humiliation: coarse men, "the dregs of the earth," will paw over his father's stock and sell it off for pennies. Is it fanciful to hear in this an image of pillage and rape? Recall that Bob has called the business his father's mistress. This business takes Bob away from his own wife, a situation he resents. How many men, he asks, spend more time with their fathers than with their wives? Bankruptcy would send the father back to his wife, and let Bob go home to his as well.

Nothing that Bob has said directly supports the conclusion that he might partially enjoy his father's defeat. Just the opposite: he has given us several explanations of why he is not resentful and why he is worried. But these explanations have a way of making us doubtful. First, his oversolicitous concern betrays the repressed wish in the vividness of its detail. Second, Bob denies feeling coerced. His father did not force Bob into the business, he simply observed, matter-of-factly, that he could no longer pay for Bob's education. Events, not the father's power, forced that decision. But we have heard this sort of denial too many times, in ways that begged to be disbelieved, for us to accept it here.

The third form that denial takes is a family legend about ambition and death. In telling this story, Bob presents his father in a light that seems inconsistent with everything else we know. The conclusion that Bob's version encourages is that his father is not a willful man, nor is he invested in the business to such a degree that its loss will destroy him. This account leaves us unpersuaded. It tells us more about what Bob needs to believe than about his father's life.

A Family Legend

In 1974 Peske Tools was a $3-million-a-year business. Bob's father was in charge of sales; Bob's uncle, the father's brother, ran the shop. At about that time two things happened that marked the beginning of a protracted, bitter feud that ended only with the uncle's death. One was that the uncle began drinking heavily. The other was that the uncle's son also joined the family business.

Bob had already been working in the plant for eight years. When his cousin began drawing a paycheck equal to his own, Bob protested. A series of skirmishes ensued. The financial details are not worth reporting; what is significant for our purpose is that, once again, favoritism became an issue. Bob saw his uncle favoring his son, raising his salary to a level that Bob had only reached after years of hard work. Characteristically, Bob attempted to treat the issue as an impartial, business matter. "I wasn't running to Daddy. I went to everyone, and said, 'Hey, I've been working here eight years. This is bullshit.'" The cousin finally quit.

At this time relations between the father and uncle were still tolerable, though fast coming apart. The uncle had begun drinking. He would sleep at work, sitting at his desk with the phone off the hook. He became increasingly unable to make the day-to-day decisions of management. Gradually Bob took over, until in all but name he was the general manager.

Eventually the father could no longer ignore the situation, and declared that he would no longer pay the uncle's salary. This was more a gesture than a literal threat, since the uncle could have easily signed his own paychecks. He did not, however. "Then he wouldn't come during the day, but he would come at night and just ghost-walk through the place. Never say a word to anyone, just walk through the place until midnight, then sit in the office until one o'clock, and then go home."

Through this time the father and uncle had been negotiating over who would buy the other out. The uncle had an inflated sense of the company's worth. Eventually, so the story goes, the father said, "Write a number on a piece of paper, and I will either pay you that, or sell for that amount." This piece of family lore is part of Bob's imagery: the idea of raging conflict settled by the flat neutrality of a number.

The uncle declined, swearing that he would destroy the company first. He began lining up customers to switch to a new company that he would form. Before this plan could materialize, however, the uncle died of a heart attack. That is, the official cause of death was heart attack. The uncle's side of the family said, "He died of a broken heart." Bob and his father were accused of pressuring him to death, and were told not to attend the funeral.

Then began another long battle, to this day not resolved, concerning the settlement. The uncle had always told his family that his share of the business was worth a million dollars; the idea that he had become a millionaire was very important to him. An independent audit, however, showed the company's net worth to be considerably less. The uncle's family accused Bob and his father of cheating them. Bob and his father maintain they complied fully with a written agreement drawn up years ago. Describing this document Bob said, "It is all very neat." Once again there is the reliance on cool, neutral factuality.

For us, the significance of this story lies in Bob's interpretation of careerism. This is a story about upward mobility, ambition, and death. Here is how Bob explains what happened to his uncle:

> If you work in a factory and expect to continue, and then get to where you are still working in a factory, kind of, except now you own it, but your entire system is set up to think like a factory worker, except now you have a big car, and paycheck, and house, it is hard to handle that success that rapidly.... There were new-found pressures that you couldn't handle by reaching into your pocket. Do we borrow a hundred thousand dollars for a new building? My uncle would say, "Oh my God, a hundred thousand dollars. Do you know how much money that is?"

Why was the father not consumed in the same way? He had come out of the same blue-collar, all-Polish neighborhood in Detroit. At one point I asked, "What did your father think of moving up in the world like that?"

B: I don't think he had much time to know, or to appreciate it. I think that was a problem for my uncle, that he couldn't cope with where he was getting. My father seemed able to cope. He was working for the future, to be independent.

RO: Not to be wealthy?

B: I don't think so. Had he become very wealthy it would have been a side benefit to being self-employed and independent.

As Bob describes him, the father has always remained just a hard-working, average guy. Something of this tone is apparent even in Bob's account of how the business grew: "They bought a piece of property in Dearborn and built a little cinderblock shop and continued to add. Built this little section and a section behind it and alongside it. Bought a building next door, then a couple next door. It just expanded over a number of years." It is an unpretentious, ramshackle sort of growth Bob describes. The uncle was obsessed with being a millionaire. The father, Bob suggests, grew rich almost by accident.

This sense of the father emerges even more clearly in contrast to the mother. She was the one, Bob says, who had an eye for the finer things. She wore stylish clothes and decorated her house as well as any interior decorator. Bob does not make her sound exactly pretentious, though he pictures her friends sniffing, "Where does she think she's coming from?" It is more that she had a certain flair. When the family moved from Poletown to the suburbs, when Bob went to a Catholic prep school, it was the mother who somehow knew that chino pants with the buckle in back were what the Grosse Pointe kids were wearing. She was the one who encouraged the children to read, and insisted that her husband learn better pronunciation.

> B: Some things my mother does with him that would drive me stark raving berserk don't bother him. Picking his clothes. My wife can't pick my clothes. My mother will tell my father, "Wear this today," and he will, not because she told him, but, "I have to wear something; I don't care what; I can wear this as easily as anything."
>
> RO: Did she respect him?
>
> B: I don't know, maybe not what I'd consider respect. She did not respect his judgment. He is not an educated man.

We are presented an image of an easy-going man—Bob at one point called him happy-go-lucky—who seems unimpressed with himself. Certainly Bob's father worked hard; if anything, he worked harder than the uncle. He wanted the independence that money would bring him, but there was no magic for him in becoming a millionaire. He moved out of the inner city when he could afford to, but he left worrying about social appearances to his wife. In some important way, Bob tells us, his father, unlike the uncle, remained detached from it all.

In the last interview a curious fact came to light. Bob has always been a poor math student. He thinks he may have been intimidated by his father's casual facility with calculus. "I thought your father was not an educated man," I said. Well, not exactly. The high school the father attended was Henry Ford Tech, at that time the Exeter of technical schools. Admission was highly competitive; those who got in were guaranteed substantial careers at Ford. The blue-collar hero turns out to have had a good share of ambition after all. Why then, we might wonder, does the main story so emphasize the father's plainspoken unpretentiousness?

Our understanding depends on seeing the relationship among several connected stories. First, there is Bob's comparison of his father and uncle. Second, we must read this comparison in the context of Bob's current fear that bankruptcy may lead to his father's death. Finally, both of these ideas are related to Bob's own career history and the role his father played in it.

A central theme of this story is that the business the father and uncle built together may end up killing both of them. It did kill the uncle, and Bob is worried that if they go bankrupt it may kill his father. The story he tells is his way of explaining why this will not happen. Stripped to its essentials, that explanation is that the uncle cared too much about becoming wealthy, while the father remained detached. The father did not get wrapped up in the business, at least not in the ultimately self-consuming way the uncle did. That is why he was able to keep his head while the uncle was losing his and, by extension, why he will not go under now if the business is lost.

I have suggested that Bob's worry about his father is exaggerated, that it is fueled by Bob's own resentment. The story he tells of the battle with the uncle supports this interpretation. First, the story explains that the father was not coercive. He did not drive the uncle out of business, he simply refused to sign his checks. Even that was not much of stand, since the uncle could have signed his own. The father did not make the uncle do anything, he simply observed, "This is the way things are, and I won't be a party to it anymore." Of course, this is exactly what he did when Bob was a student. He said, "I am not willing to pay for you any more." From everything we have heard, Bob did feel coerced at the time, though he denies it now. The story of the uncle denies that the father was coercive in that battle and, by extension, in the struggle with Bob himself.

Second, the account of the struggle with the uncle denies that the father was unfair. It pictures the father as the essence of fairness. The uncle would name a figure, and the father would choose whether to buy him out or sell out himself. The settlement after the uncle's death was managed by an outside auditor. We have heard Bob talk about unfairness in his own dealings with his father. What he says about this is ambiguous. Sometimes he suggests that his father is scrupulously impartial when one might hope for a little parental favoritism. Sometimes he says that his father pretends to be impartial but ends up favoring his sister. The story of the uncle explains to us that the father is not an unfair man.

Finally, the story of the uncle explains that the father is not an ambitious man and he is not wedded to his business. This too bears on Bob's situation. Bob has not been able to build a career of his own, to be ambitious in his own right, because he is his father's employee. Further, Bob is wedded to his father's career. He tells us that he does not get to spend enough time with his wife because he is spending too much time with his father's "mistress." The account of the uncle corrects this impression too. It explains that this business is not an all-consuming thing. It did not take over the father's life, and did not take over Bob's life either. Ambition was not that important to the father, or to Bob himself.

In each of these stories it is as if Bob is answering a question that he does not consciously acknowledge has been asked. It is as if he were saying, "You might think that I resent my father because he was unfair and coercive, and forced me into a business that took over my life and never let me have a career of my own. You might think that I would be just as happy to see him get his comeuppance now if this company folds. But you are wrong. He was not any of those things, not with my uncle, and not with me." We may wonder who is being reassured.

To return now to the larger perspective of this study, both the problem in Bob's own career, and the rationalizing story he tells of his father and uncle, are framed by the now-familiar terms of career culture—impersonality and career trajectory. Bob differs from previous cases in that he has not been able to use his own career as a way of changing who he is in relation to his father. Therefore, he tells a story of his father's career that changes the father's history and, in the process, the meaning of Bob's career as well. In some ways Bob is like Ben. Ben was unable to allow himself aggressive commitment to a career; Bob's career is thwarted by external events. Both men seem to suffer an inhibition of aggression. The nature of their inhibition differs: oversimplifying matters somewhat, Ben cannot allow himself to be aggressive, while Bob seems beaten down by circumstances. Perhaps for that reason each of them suffers two related problems. Each is concerned about his potential for destructiveness. And each is curiously uninvolved in his own career. Ben is "bored" and Bob wants to retire. In some ways they remind us of Don, who also worries about his potential destructiveness, and who also seems more worried than pleased by his last promotion.

The idea of solving an internalized relationship by changing the other person—instead of changing oneself—has certain apparent limits. It does not work psychodynamically. Although Bob tries to protect his father, unlike Ken, Al, or Mike, who counterattack, he does not end up feeling any closer to him. Bob is invested in preserving a fiction of his father, one that denies the aggression in their relationship. This fiction does not fulfill even its defensive function. Bob remains anxious about his father's health. We suspect that Bob's own inadequately repressed fantasy is the danger he dimly recognizes.

Beyond its defensive insufficiency, Bob's fiction of his father has another cost. It denies the assertive meaning of careers. What Bob denies about his father's career is also what he denies about his own. Bob needs a life work that will allow him his own assertive independence. If he could come to terms with that portion of what career means, he might be willing to acknowledge his father's willfulness too.

The strategy that Bob employs involves a story, a family legend. It is in some ways like the stories Ben tells of the men in his family. Now we may ask, just how damaging is this? Suppose I had not come along with my tape recorder? In that case Bob might never have told this story. We may agree that the story reveals something about what Bob needs to believe about his life, but it is harder to argue that this self-understanding influences his life. It is diagnostic, not self-formative. But suppose the situation were otherwise. Suppose Bob not only told himself a story about his father, but lived his own life in such a way as to make the story true. In that case the story would not simply be a way that we might learn something about him, it would have a formative influence on the person he has come to be. With this idea, we pass to the last case.

11

A Risky Life

Lew is a big bear of a guy with a loud, gruff voice and an oddly uncertain manner. He sprawls back in the chair, speaking in that loud voice with unusual candor. Yet for all his plainspokenness there remains a peculiar hesitation.

After a while most interviewees become comfortable with this strange business. Standing in the kitchen, waiting for the coffee water to boil, we can joke casually. The taped interviews always remain a bit more formal than the chit-chat on either side of them. With Lew, the reverse is true. The interviews feel unusually revealing, but standing around afterward he seems not quite sure what to say.

His first words, before we get the tape rolling, are, "I just got back from spelunking this weekend." Spelunking, he explains, is cave exploring. Later he tells me that he likes to entertain people with the adventurousness of his life.

Lew has held a series of jobs in health administration over the last six years. His background, however, is in neither public health nor administration, but in theater and communication. Before coming to Ann Arbor he worked as a disc jockey in Philadelphia. He is notably and proudly unqualified for the job he now holds—he is in charge of liason among several cooperating health agencies—and not at all inclined to collect the union card of a master's degree in health administration, even though it would allow him the freedom to move. He has worked his way to a position of unusual responsibility based only, he says, "on a loud voice and an ability to sell a line of bullshit."

Lew said he likes his job, yet had been thinking seriously of shifting back to radio or acting or possibly union organizing. Any of these choices would be reasonable. He has been an actor as well as a disc jockey. Union work offers a unique synthesis of his talents and interests: "It is not the same as getting up in front of a microphone or a camera, but it has the same appeal... getting up in front of people, getting them stirred up and motivated... almost like a campaign. What unions do is campaign all the time."

If the choices Lew imagined match his past experience and talent, it bears mentioning that 1983 was an extraordinarily bad time for anyone in Michigan to think about leaving a secure job. At the time of my interviews with him,

Michigan's social service system was reeling from budget cutbacks. No job was secure. Lew, who does not have a formal degree in any social service related field, would have found it very difficult to land another position comparable to the one he was holding. On the other hand, Lew had become president of the union and, for that reason, had the highest seniority of anyone. While virtually every other public health administrator in the state must have been wondering if the next budget cut would erase his or her job, Lew was secure. That security would have disappeared the moment he left that position. Still, he thought of moving on.

A popular Detroit beer company—"the beer for the man who looks deep inside and finds something different"—begins its TV ad with a sturdy young man intoning, "When I gave up my job with the airline to start my own company, a lot of people told me I was making a mistake." Of course he succeeds: the mustache on his lip and the pretty girl on his arm leave no doubt. Lew, who exemplifies the ethic, says,

> It really does not take a whole lot of ingenuity to do what you want, because everyone else is fearful.... You are one step ahead of everyone else who is afraid. They take one or two or three major risks in their life and that is it. And a lot of times they regret it the rest of their lives, and don't know how to move away from it.... I like risky people who assert [themselves for] what they want.... They seek out the things that make them happy.

What does the risky life represent to Lew? Gradually, it became clear that it is his escape from a dismal alternative—a life of anxious, depressed paralysis. His first job after graduate school was as an actor in a one-man traveling show.

> I would drive to some school, set myself up, perform, pack everything up, drive to another school, perform, sometimes two, three, four times a day, then find myself a motel or drive to the next city and find a motel, and do the thing all over again. I did that for five months, and I succeeded. I blew an engine in the car and got another one. Sometimes I ran out of money and had to sleep in my car. I really just pitted myself against the worst conditions.... It gave me the sense that I was a good survivor.

Being a good survivor is important to Lew. For years he doubted himself; now the risky life is his way of proving his mettle. Lew was the first among his friends in the theater department at college to try for a professional job in summer stock. "Let me describe what it is like being an actor. It is a very difficult experience for someone who is not sure of himself. You have to sell yourself. A constant, repetitious selling yourself. And I had been the first in my peer group to take that step, to go out and look for a job. I broke the ice here too. And I was proud of myself." The constant selling recalls what he said of union organizing. Acting in general, and getting that first job, are in the style of campaigning.

He had planned to try out for bit parts, but the company director encouraged him to audition for the lead. Never one to back away from a challenge, Lew tried for the part, got it, and did creditably well for his first professional performance. At the same time he became involved with the woman who played the female lead.

> I was working with this woman who just saw through my ability. She said, "This guy can't do it." Every chance she put me down. . . . I took so much grief from this woman that for the rest of the summer I was in a depression, the most serious I have ever had . . . this feeling that I will never be able to support myself. . . . She had her own problems; she was heavily on tranquilizers. . . . The irony of it was that she was also coming on to me. We started seeing each other, and she was just as caustic and malicious personally as she was on stage. But I was challenged. It had become like a life-or-death situation.

After the season ended he went home. He describes a period of intense depression that lasted about a month, and then a characteristic escape by way of decisive movement.

> When I say "depressed," I mean I woke up and it hit me. I'd spend the day alienated from everything going on. . . . I would just walk in a daze. . . . And then I survived again. I got in this new Volkswagen that my brother gave me, which I didn't know how to drive. He gave me a fifteen-minute lesson and said, "Okay, you are on your own." I drove to Atlantic City, where I knew some people who were working on a Shakespeare festival . . . and got a job in about a day.

Once again he recovers by way of movement; jumping in a car that he can barely drive, with no money in his pocket, and landing on his feet. But let us back up. A woman has entered the piece, a woman who "had her hang-ups" but who nevertheless intimidated him. She and her various sisters reappear in Lew's life. Sometimes he emphasizes their neurotic helplessness, other times he fears that they will unmask him.

That winter he moved to Philadelphia, got a job at a radio station, and started dating the woman who did the morning news. When the station was sold they moved to Ann Arbor together.

> Carol wanted to get her strength back together. We were unemployed three months. I managed to get odd jobs, but she was incapacitated, so she wanted to build up some confidence. . . .
> Both of us had lost our jobs, but I am a resourceful person. Although I was depressed . . . I don't sit around moping about it. I do something, even if it is not what I want to do. It keeps me interested and involved.

As it happens, Carol eventually moved to Hawaii. Lew, who had planned to move with her to the coast, stayed behind. As he tells the story, however, he emphasizes Carol's depressive lethargy, his own energy. When acting seemed a dead-end, Lew again moved on, decisively.

> I didn't see myself growing [in radio] so ... I went down to CETA and told them, "I want to do a career change; I don't know in what. I think social service might be something I'd like to try." I applied to one job, told them I had no credentials. But what I had learned in my previous background was how to act. I can sell a line of bullshit real well.... I didn't get in initially, but the woman they hired quit the first day and they called me.

He held the job a year and a half, then applied to be director when the spot opened. "I came in a squeaky second to an MSW. I said to myself, "I think I have reached my ceiling here, better start looking around." I made a few phone calls, got hired by the Mental Health Center in a new program. Six months down the line the coordinator [a woman] left and I got promoted as the coordinator."

Again, notice the contrast between himself and women. Women mope, they lose confidence, they quit after one day. Lew acts, lands on his feet, and carries off the job despite his lack of training. However, it soon emerged that women are more dangerous figures in Lew's life than these portraits of helplessness suggest. Even when they are neurotic, women threaten to call his bluff. That first summer stock acting job ended in despair. There have been other similar occasions.

Lew's first performances in graduate school were tremendously successful. At the same time he was flunking out of school. Once again he was involved with a woman who threatened to see through him.

> There was this older woman I wanted to impress. If I had thought about it, she was impressed anyway. She had her own hang-ups. But two or three times I just wasn't able to do it with her, and it scared me: "Is this an indication that I am gay?" ... [I felt] I could never do as well again as I did on the first performance of that play. I feared every night it would get worse.... I still have this fear that if someone took a good look at me they would see a sham. I am still scared that it is not real. Every year I think less of that.

Eventually I asked whether his fear of being uncovered entered into his sexual relations. He said, "Well, let me tell you how I impressed her. It was all the preliminaries. I don't think I ever really screwed her.... It was the initial sample that was outstanding."

The big initial impression and the inadequate follow-through are the themes of still another early job. His first summer home from college, Lew talked a tool and die company into hiring him as a draftsman. At first all went well. Lew took on more sophisticated assignments than the owner expected him to handle, and carried them off successfully. Still, his drawing on more basic projects remained a shade imprecise. "So he kept me doing the basic stuff, over and over again. And the anxiety of having to do this, and coming to work, was too much. . . . I began to feel claustrophobic, a real heavy sense of being trapped."

Although in this case it is a man who threatens to unmask Lew, the danger is the same. This last passage draws a connection between two fears in Lew's life: of being discovered a fraud, and feeling trapped, immobile. When the drafting boss threatened to discover Lew's marginal competence—once again he had talked his way into a job for which he was not really qualified—Lew became not only anxious, but claustrophobic.

Lew's answer to the fear of paralysis is counterphobic motility. His answer to the threat of being unmasked is to uncover the ineffectuality and sham in others. His descriptions of women emphasize their inability to meet a challenge. More generally, he has a caustic eye for the pretensions of people around him. He recalls an incident with his boss when he worked one summer at a bank. "This supervisor covered a book with brown paper, but so accurately that it took two or three hours. I said, "I hope you are going to read that book, because you are sure taking a lot of care with it." It was obviously one of the first hardcover books he'd bought; I couldn't see him reading it."

Then there was the young woman at work who went to Barnard. Lew tried to strike up a conversation with her, not out of romantic interest, but simply because "I thought I could talk with her, because I read a lot. But she gave me the impression she had no time, or wasn't interested. She wasn't really an educated person. She was doing a mechanical job. She wasn't really a thinker." If Lew fears being the object of damning scrutiny, he is also an expert at seeing through others. His is a sardonic, piercing gaze.

To sum up what we have heard so far: Although Lew is often afraid that he is not competent, he takes on exceptional challenges and seems to deliberately court risk. He is often afraid that someone, especially a woman, will see through him. In apparent defense, he is quick to see through the pretensions of others. When he does feel beaten down or depressed he feels immobilized. He restores himself by decisive movement. Overall, his is a style of attacking danger head-on. The meaning of these themes lies in his childhood history.

Lew's parents married late, after a long courtship. The father was thirty-seven when he married; he was forty-three when Lew was born. Before his marriage the father was a musician. Lew believes that his father married ambivalently and never made his peace with the decision. In fact, he disappeared for two years shortly after the marriage to live with another woman. Even after he returned he spent much of his time out of the house, involved in a dozen local political organizations and causes. Lew recalls his mother complaining about his endless "outside interests."

The mother, who might once have appeared romantically sensitive, had by middle age become a nagging, fear-ridden woman who depressed everyone around her. The father escaped to his outside organizations when he could. (Lew, who never actually witnessed this part of the father's life, imagines him as a passionate orator.) When he was trapped at home the father absented himself emotionally. He was forever preoccupied with his music or a crossword puzzle. When these escapes failed he walked around distractedly in what Lew describes as an "anxiety cloud." Meanwhile the mother nagged and worried; Lew recalls that she fed on misfortune. "I remember one woman who was having a divorce, and gravitated toward my mother because my mother dealt with tragedy. Then when this woman started stabilizing, my mother was still dealing with the tragedy, and this woman didn't want to deal with it anymore. My mother couldn't understand that."

Over the years, Lew's mother gradually became house-ridden by anxiety. For a time she taught school, but the school children made her too nervous and she had to quit. Later she took a job two blocks from the house. Lew recalls her saying, "Thank God it isn't any further, because you know I can't take the bus."

The mother brought her sense of impending disaster to everyone in the family. Lew says, "It was always 'look out,' because around any corner there might be another catastrophe." When Lew's fourteen-year-old brother, Paulie, wanted to play high school football, the mother refused to sign the letter of permission—too dangerous. Football can be a dangerous game, but Joey was a big, aggressive kid. At the time he was living with his uncle in California, because his exploits as a run-away, gang leader and car thief had become too much for his parents' patience. He probably could have handled linebacker.

Lew recalls his mother's reaction when he got into Brooklyn Tech, one of a handful of elite high schools in New York. Lew took a special examination to get in, succeeded, and called his mother with the good news.

> I remember the first words out of her mouth were something like, "Are you sure you can do it?" It wasn't like a pat on the back, or "My son did so well." . . . What I was left with after the phone call was, "God, I made a mistake. I shouldn't have accepted going to this school." She scared me all the time. I always had a sense of fear about what I did. Because I was stubborn I would take on risky things, but I never enjoyed what I did because I was always so fucking scared. I carried that almost into my middle twenties, this fear of life.

In a later passage he describes the perpetual self-doubt that became his own internal refrain.

> There was a lot of internal talking. Could I do this or not? A ping-pong game. A simple thing like a date. Could I go out with this person? I would build a case. "Yes I can." Then I'd build a case, "No." It was a constant rumination. I'd never let myself go. Never a simple thought, always pulling it apart. "No, you can't do that. Who are you kidding? Yes you can; no you can't."

By this point we can see a good deal of what the risky life means to Lew. Lew prefers to see himself as his father's son, the impulsive romantic, not the child of his anxious, nagging mother. Here too we find an explanation for his association of defeat and claustrophobia. Lew's mother, a figure of chronic depression, was house-ridden. His father had traded away a romantic musician's career and now seemed trapped in a dreary marriage. Vitality was pictured in escape. Lew is resolved not to make his father's mistake. Speaking of the choices now before him, he says:

> I am really beginning to miss the creative part of my life, the acting. . . . I see my father becoming the amateur musician, you know, going from this whole sense of becoming a professional. . . . It sort of means a defeat for me . . . that the next step is that I am going to find me a woman who will drive me into the clouds. And I think there is a lot of fear, even though I don't express it a lot, that that may happen to me. . . . I don't think my father ever truly made the commitment.

The symbolism of movement and the risky life is defined by the contrast between Lew's mother and father. The expressive, unstructured life is the father's portion; nagging anxiety and immobility go with the mother. She cannot drive, take the bus, or manage a job more than two blocks from home. In contrast, the pleasure of the father's life is defined as "outside activity."

This portion of what challenge and movement mean to Lew are ideas that he himself has expressed. There are other connections that he may be more reluctant to consider in detail, although even these are ideas he occasionally mentions. He admits that there are some things he simply prefers to let lie; otherwise "It is like opening a can of snakes."

There is strong evidence that Lew has an investment in protecting the image of his father as a romantic figure. In fact, it seems that the whole family, with the exception of the mother, conspired in building a family myth.

Lew has built a world of fantasy around the father's oblique references to another, happier time. He pictures his father hanging out in the coffeehouses of Greenwich Village in the thirties and forties, discussing Schopenhauer and the Communist Manifesto with intellectual friends, writing a bit of poetry. In Lew's mind the details of this time are indistinct; they have the soft focus of myth.

> Sitting around in the coffee shops with the same pair of pants on, and shoes, living in a one- or two-room flat in the Village with two or three other people. The books they read were great works of Kant, that kind of stuff. Playing music, being articulate, knowledgeable about art and poetry. That is my image. They had a lot of fun together; they partied a lot. A lot of my images come from [old photos], and little pieces my father would tell me.

Apparently the father encouraged the illusion; Lew recalls, "he would give me little hints." Lew explained, "He used to hint around. I got the impression he was always doing other things. I don't know where I got it. Maybe I thought he was still sitting in the coffee shops."

Interestingly enough, Lew's brother, Paulie, also made up stories about the father. For years Paulie told his friends that his father was a banker, though he actually sold pharmaceuticals. Only the mother refused to play the game. "My mother used to put my father down all the time, degrade him. 'Oh, your father does this, he is never home, he is finally making a living. He spends more time showing his affections to other people. He never brings anything home.'"

Does Lew himself believe the myth? Certainly he has tried. At the same time there is always a doubt in his mind. At one point he remarked, "Maybe I needed to make my father mysterious." This discussion soon led to the question of whether Lew actually respected his father. As Lew now sees it, the reason he created the romantic image was connected to his doubts about his father. "What didn't you respect?" I asked.

> His relationship with my mother. The fact that I was getting a lot of shit from her, and he seemed to take a lot of shit from her and sort of resigned himself to it. He would storm out of the house at times. But he seemed to deal with it by being away, out of the house or into himself.... I would get "I'll give you money but don't tell your mother. Don't tell your mother we did this." Not that we did anything unusual. A lot of times he would start off the conversation with, "Don't tell your mother I told you this."

A few minutes later Lew began telling me a story about Paulie. Paulie, it seems, was not an angel. He was in a gang. He stole a car and ran away to Florida. He shot a BB gun at Lew, and once came at him with a knife. He was arrested several times, and stabbed a man in the Navy. Yet, though he made life unnaturally interesting for Lew, Paulie redeemed himself by a sense of fraternal loyalty that was magnificently direct. When Lew got himself in trouble with the bullies at school, Paulie passed the word. "The word got out that Paulie was going to kill anyone who beat me up, so nobody touched me. It was like the tide went out."

Another time, at summer camp, Lew was burned through the carelessness of a counselor. "My brother then—this was never proven—burned down the bunk, the entire cabin, with his football uniform in it. I remember the camp directors made me lie to my mother and say it was my fault. They told me to say I had burned myself playing with matches. And it didn't come out until several years later; I think my brother told them."

The contrast between Paulie and the father is stark. His father offered no protection. Paulie was terrifying, but when Lew needed him he was effective. Significantly, Lew remembers the counselors' admonition, "Don't tell your mother." Lew's ineffective father had the same refrain.

Lew recalls how his father would try to build up his confidence. "He'd say, 'You're tall, you have lots of attributes. Why are you insecure?' I was just indecisive about whether to believe him. It was hard for me to say, 'Oh, you're right Dad.' I doubted his knowledge; I didn't doubt his sincerity. There must have been a part of me that just didn't respect him."

These last passages force us to reconsider our first, simple understanding of the case. At first it seemed that Lew drew a contrast between his adventurous father and his fear-ridden mother. This still seems true, but now we begin to see that Lew exaggerated his father's adventurousness and ignored the ways he was ineffectual.

Earlier I said that Lew fears being unmasked. In counterattack, he is quick to point out the frailties of others. However, there is another side to Lew's piercing gaze. If Lew sees deeply and acidly, he also keeps his opinions to himself. He is more than quiet; he is sealed off from the world.

> I lived with a guy for a year and a half. Once he said, "How come you never talk to me?" I saw myself as talking all the time, in my head. I had a running dialogue with myself, but I didn't let any of it out.... Most of my life as a younger person was seen from inside, like encased in a shell. Walking around with this piece of translucent concrete around me.... I always felt I was seeing what was going on around me.... I was collecting images of people. On the subway, I would see how people read, how they farted, how they fidgeted around.

If Lew saw through the pretensions of others—and he did, constantly—he kept his opinions to himself. This silence makes sense as an attempt to preserve his father's dignity. Lew's mother, remember, was always disparaging the father. She would say, in effect, "Your father talks a big game, but he is really a phony." Lew, who shared his mother's doubts, could not afford to feel that both parents were inadequate, and so he refused to admit to himself what he actually suspected. His piercing, unmasking gaze is turned away from his father, but inevitably it finds other targets against whom he directs the scorn he cannot direct at his father.

These observations alter our understanding of Lew's identification with his father as well. It first seemed that Lew emulated his father in order to be unlike his mother, to be adventurous rather than depressively immobilized. Now it appears that Lew's identification is with a very one-sided fiction of his father. The father with whom Lew identifies is not the one he saw around the house every day, but instead, the father of a romantic past, or of those mysterious outside activities.

This business of disavowing what one knows is difficult. We have seen that Lew cannot stop looking, and so he turns his sardonic gaze away from his father toward substitute targets. It seems that this was not enough, and so Lew enlisted a second line of defense. He levels the accusations that should go against his father against himself. Instead of saying that his father is a sham,

Lew fears that he himself is. Instead of letting his mother see through his father, Lew now feels that a string of women are ready to see through him. Even Lew's description of his silence may fit here. Where his father walked around in "an anxiety cloud," Lew describes walking around "with a piece of translucent concrete around me."

Lew's conscious identification is with the father of romantic myth. There seems to be an unconscious identification with the real, disappointing father as well. Lew has turned himself into the sham he suspects his father of having been. Now it is Lew who must fear exposure. We suspect that the deeper danger Lew fears is not his own unmasking, but the chance that he might see through his father. Lew's piercing, sardonic gaze now seems to be displaced from its true object, the father, onto a series of intellectually and artistically pretentious proxies.

Lew obviously pays a price for all of this. Much of the time he feels incompetent and vulnerable to exposure. Why would he go to these lengths, turning himself into a copy of what he despises in his father? One reason is that Lew's father seems too vulnerable, and Lew cannot afford to lose him. The adventurous father is really Lew's only model for adult competence. The second reason is that Lew seems to have been afraid, if only indistinctly, of his own disappointment and capacity for violent anger.

How much did he have to fear? We must consider not only what Lew knew about himself, but also the models his family provided of rage gone amok. There was Paulie: gang leader, thief, arsonist. Paulie was thrown out of the Navy for stabbing a man. Eventually he murdered his wife and committed suicide. Lew tries to explain Paulie's life:

> Paulie's wife kept saying, "You know, this is related to all the anger you feel. You know, your father is dead. You never resolved any of it, the anger toward your mother or your father." My brother and I, we had never talked about it! I wasn't aware of my own yet, and his was channeled into this real hatred toward society.... And of course he died before he ever recognized it, or maybe he did recognize it and couldn't handle it. I really have no idea. Maybe she got to places he didn't want to be gotten to.... Because I was angry with my father. He was really pretty ineffectual in terms of getting in between my mother and her vibes.

We have no way of knowing whether Lew is right about his brother. For our purposes Paulie remains only another voice in which Lew tells his own story. What Lew tells us about himself by way of his explanation of his brother is that Paulie acted out the anger both brothers felt, probably toward both parents. Expressed in the raw colors that were Paulie's style, that rage led to murder and suicide. Lew took the other road, toward the emotional deadening of the concrete bubble.

Did Lew fear the same rage in himself? During his first year in graduate school the pressure of acting became intolerable. Eventually he checked himself into a psychiatric hospital. As his parents finally drove him home, Lew, now semidelusional, imagined the police were chasing him to pay for a water bill. Back at home, Lew entered a period of depression and irritability: "It was just a real strange part of my life. I was not getting along with my parents.... I almost choked someone; I tackled him. That was the beginning of heavy acting-out toward my parents. I fought the draft and got out. The psychiatrist said I would kill—the wrong people."

Usually the low periods in Lew's life begin with the fear of incompetence, often provoked by feeling unmasked, and lead to depression. He describes that depression in terms of lethargy and also what he calls "alienation," feeling sealed-off from others. Now we see that his numb isolation is itself a defense against seeing too sharply, too accusingly, and acting out his anger.

Lew's father died while Lew was in Philadelphia. The family had moved to Florida eight months before. He died of a heart attack the night after playing a concert.

> I have pictures taken of him the night before he died, playing the violin. And I look at them, at his face—they are close enough—trying to see any signs that he is going to die. There is an intensity to the way he played the violin, and I am looking at his face, knowing that in the middle of the night he died.
>
> I got ready to go down there on my own. I told a friend across the street, and another friend. Just a strange kind of drifting sense until I got down there.... My mother was distraught. And I was a mixture of being an observer and being emotionally involved in the sadness and loss. I was sort of drifting.
>
> I didn't want to deal with my mother's grief, and I didn't believe my mother. I believed she was hurt and lonely and upset, but I think I was angry at her. My experiences of my parents were always of them yelling at each other. And now here is my mother wailing that she has lost her husband, and I wanted to tell her to stop acting. It seemed genuine ... but I knew that my mother was crying for herself more than my father.... I just remember my anger toward her ... feeling, "Why is my mother grieving so much? She didn't like him when he was alive." She always belittled him and put him down.

Here is the way I understand Lew's reaction. The anger he feels for his mother's wailing is displaced. Lew is asking himself, "What do I really feel?" Certainly there is grief, but there is also frustration, hope finally lost of ever touching this father whose enthusiasm was reserved for a life Lew could never share. Looking at the photo, Lew attempts to find not only what passion killed his father, but also the glow of his mysterious "outside" life. Who was he, this father? What did he really love? These questions, and the angry frustration that accompanies them, are blocked. And that is why Lew snarls to himself, "She didn't love him when he was alive."

> I felt numb. All my life I had felt like this alien in this nucleus of strange people. And when my father died I still felt that. I didn't feel very real about myself, and in tap with other people. I still felt in a box. When I came down there—you know the book *The Stranger?* They are burying his mother and he is following and he doesn't know what to feel. I felt that way. I remember the anger toward my mother, and a real sense of loss.

Lew and I spoke eight years after his father had died, absorbed in his private passion, seven years after Paulie's life had ended in a blood-spattered room, almost six years after Carol had left for Hawaii. The last few years, Lew says, have felt like a vacation. He knows that he is ignoring some things. He even acknowledges that he may pay a price in intimacy by holding himself in reserve. Still, the last years have felt more stable. The old compulsive quality of risk-taking has settled into something more deliberate.

> I don't feel as intimate as I can be, or would like to be. There is a lid on my emotions. But I feel I'd better let it rest. It is hard to describe the feeling of constantly going over in your head why you can or can't do things. When you don't have that conflict you want to just leave it rest. It's like a den of snakes; you open the wrong lid and it's going to come out at you. I know I have boxed myself into a structure that keeps me content, whereas I used to have a blind sense of risk. I would take risks because I felt I had to. For me to drop my job and go to California would be taking a big risk that might open up a can of snakes. So I know there is a lid.

In this passage several themes come together. Lew still values risky movement, even though here he acknowledges that he has become more sedentary. In another interview he describes himself as "ponderous." There is a change, of course. His early moves now seem like blind motion; at one point he pictured himself as bouncing from one thing to another with no real plan or understanding. Now his actions feel more deliberate and effective. Yet this is a limited change. He still thinks longingly of California, he still admires the life-style of the man who pursues whatever will make him happy. The quality of movement has changed, but not its significance.

I find the scene of Lew staring at his father's photograph, trying to detect the mysterious passion that he never shared with his family and that now has removed him forever, the most poignant of this story. We have heard other cases where fathers seemed irretrievably lost. Ken, Al and Mike, the three men who follow the high road of trajectory, each feels unrecognized by his father. This is not surprising: the point of trajectory is to leave home far behind.

In Lew's case we might have expected something different. He too uses trajectory to leave one parent—his mother. However, adventurous mobility is part of his identification with his father. They share a bond. Why then, at the end, does Lew feel once again numb, detached, alienated? The answer, of course, is that Lew's identification has not been with the father of real life, but with a romantic myth. This symbolic father has been purged of ambiguity. The shadings of admiration and contempt, love and anger, that Lew felt toward his real father do not register on this half-tone symbolic image.

This is not to say that the symbolic father is a simple representation. He must be interpreted with reference to everyone else in the family. The father's romantic history is back-lit by the mother's depressive anxiety. His ineffectual placating is defined in contrast to Paulie's violence. His activity outside the home and before the marriage is important because of the suspicion, fanned by the mother, that he really is a failure. In short, the significance of the father is only given by his location in the larger company of the family. However, within this larger context, the father represents unambiguously one set of virtues— adventurous independence.

By accepting this version of his father, Lew evades a set of troubling questions. Why could the father not rescue the family from Paulie's violence, the mother's pessimism, his own anxiety? Why, in short, was he not more of a father? Lew's answer is that his father really was heroic—somewhere else. The alternative would be to accept his mother's view that the father was an old fool of a dreamer who abandoned his family once and might do so again. To save his father from his own agreement with this assessment, Lew collaborates with the romantic myth. Later, in his own life, he plays out a career that preserves this interpretation of what it means to be a man. The risky life saves Lew from thinking too much about how he really feels about his father.

However, the myth exacts a cost. Lew cannot totally escape the suspicion that his father really was inadequate. Identification with the heroic myth is accompanied by its invidious alternative. Unconsciously, Lew also identifies with the father he holds in contempt.

Lew fears that he himself is inadequate. Career becomes a perpetual trial by fire, tossing aside hard-won security for a new risk. Fearful of replicating his father's marriage, Lew has remained single. He is not comfortable with his independence, but he seems unable to sustain a relationship. Finally, no job ever measures up to the vividness Lew expects of life. Though he works hard and well, Lew lives for his adventurous weekends. His friends talk interminably of their ordinary jobs; Lew talks about spelunking. He is the adventurer of his circle. Sometimes, though, he wonders why there is nothing in his life that he finds interesting enough to talk about for hours at a time.

In the year or two before our interviews took place a change had been occurring. As we know, Lew takes great pride in his ability to move into a job for which he is unqualified and carry it off successfully. Here, both his willingness to take risks and his talent as an actor are important. Lew feels that the same training that made him an actor, his keen power of observation and his ability to grasp the telling detail, allow him to decipher the rules of organizations. This ability to get to the essence of things quickly makes him a particularly effective administrator. He feels he has the street savvy to see through the obfuscations of bureaucracies. At the same time, there has been a change. These days, Lew says, he is more aware that one cannot run an organization simply on an actor's charisma.

> Because I can get to the essence... the details will come as I go along. And what I have realized is that I still need the details, you can't just know the essence. And where the rough edges were before is that I wasn't ready to grasp the details.... You know, in any field there is a whole language that is used. There are people who communicate to each other in that language.... You have to know how to convey [information]. You convey that in a language people understand.... I may be able to perceive, but if I want to function in that field I have to convey what I perceive. And much of that detail is the common language.

Lew has always brought his identity of actor to the jobs he holds. As an actor he is both more observant and less engaged than the people around him. Recently he has started to feel his own isolation. His big theatrical manner is starting to give way to something more like the common speech of daily commerce. Once again, our clue is the story he tells of his father. Toward the end of our last interview Lew offered a revised version of his father's career. His father, Lew said, really enjoyed being a salesman.

> I think that what my father eventually did in his life was to get to the nitty-gritty and actually apply himself to a trade. And although he still liked the showmanship aspects, essentially he was a salesman.... He was not ashamed of it at all. He would say, "People like me to come into their stores. They look forward to it." And yet I liked the drama, the fantasy stuff.

The contrast here is between the showmanship of the mythical father, acknowledged here to be largely Lew's invention, and a practical career based on a lively interpersonal touch. The key word is "nitty-gritty." It is the opposite of Lew's own showy style. Just before this passage Lew had said, "I like the show, the cream. I have spent my whole life siphoning off the cream. I will do clinical work up to a point. As soon as it gets to the nitty-gritty, where I really have to apply clinical skills, I'll back off."

In an organization dedicated to providing service, Lew's role makes him both more and less than everyone else. He is the administrator, but he is not really a clinician. The quality of his membership is still limited to that of a very good actor.

Yet as I noted, things are changing. Lew may continue to become less of a charismatic outsider, more of an ordinary participant. If he does, we may expect him to continually reinterpret the significance of his father's career.

Part Five

Conclusion

12

The Theater of Careers

One way to summarize what I have been saying throughout this study is that careers provide men with a kind of theater. A man's career provides him with a vehicle through which he attempts to answer the question, "What have I made of myself?" This theater is created out of the alliance of two partners. Its outer form is organized by the dominant preoccupations of career culture: career advancement and impersonality. These two themes define the horizon of men's experience, what they expect of themselves, how they behave, and how they explain themselves. However, what men enact and explain within the dramaturgical conventions of careers goes far beyond work itself; it includes lifelong preoccupations about themselves and their relations to others. These meanings are not publicly acknowledged. They are disavowed by the alliance of individual, psychodynamic suppression and membership in a common culture that agrees to accept some explanations as sufficient and not inquire further.

In each of the cases presented here I have tried to show the psychodynamic subtext of life stories presented and enacted within the conventions of career culture. In each case we began with a man's current, conscious experience and worked backward toward themes that are biographically older and less readily acknowledged. This way of presenting things makes clear what men have in common—their shared membership in the culture of careers, with its expectations and rationalizations. At the same time, it suggests that their private motives may be quite disparate. The common tongue in which they all speak appears primarily to hide their idiosyncrasies, and to an extent, it does. One of the conclusions of this study must be that men deploy the formulas of careerism toward quite different ends. But it is also true that many of these men share not only what they will publicly admit, but what they each attempt to conceal. In this last chapter I would like to bring these seven men together once again to show what they have in common, this time however, building forward from their psychodynamic motives toward their public behavior. This will be, necessarily, a considerable simplification. These men really are quite different. Yet to the extent that we can describe what they share we will also see what kind of psychosocial engine careerism is.

Bearing in mind, then, the substantial variations among them, five of these men describe their families—and especially their fathers—in similar terms. Ken, Al, Mike, Ben, and Bob all say that they often felt bullied, frightened, and humiliated by their fathers. The range among them is considerable. Bob felt passively coerced; his father did not whip him, but stood waiting for him to "smell the belt." Mike was physically abused. The others fill in the middle range. These men also say that they felt unable to be close to their fathers; they picture their fathers as at best distant, at worst jealous and emotionally erratic. Here again the range is considerable. Bob's father was too busy; sometimes Bob felt that his father was disappointed in him. Al's father was cold. Ken, Mike, and Ben describe their fathers as more actively disapproving and recall that their attempts at affection were met with unpredictable anger and jealousy.

These childhood experiences have led most of these men to turn their adult careers into scenes of a repetitive drama. With the exception of Bob, each of them attempts to find in work a substitute for the affection and recognition that he missed when he was younger. Ken offers his protégé what his own father never offered him, Al hopes that Spencer will give him the recognition and approval that his father withheld, Mike tries to be affectionate with his customers, and Ben does the same with his students. None of these overtures work out, partly because they are unrealistic—they demand too much—but partly because even as these men extend the invitation they turn it into an occasion for rejection and humiliation. When rejection comes or, perhaps more exactly, when these men perceive in ordinary indifference the very insult they fear, they retreat into aggressive self-defense. At this moment, career culture provides a formula of self-restoration. One half of this formula—trajectory—encourages aggressive self-aggrandizement. The other aspect of the formula—the detachment of self-in-role—allows men to say, in effect, "I never really cared in the first place."

Three men—Ken, Mike, and Al—present this syndrome in its purest form. Ben presents a similar psychodynamic dilemma but, for various reasons, he is unable to make use of the aggressive solution that ambition offers. Bob, who mentions some of the same themes as the others, though in notably less extreme form, seems to have different adult preoccupations. I will return to him in a moment.

One striking feature that unites these men is their declared interest in the social aspect of their work. Ken prides himself on being "a coach," Mike describes his cadre of employees as "a family," Al suggests that he is more a "counselor" than a salesman, and Ben tells his class stories about his own life because he believes effective teaching requires personal engagement. Of the group, only Bob holds back. Although he recognizes that running a factory depends on personal contact, he is much less enthusiastic than the others about the social politics of business.

This investment in the social give-and-take of work is itself surprising. Sociological research, from Sutton to Sofer and Kanter, portrays a more overtly impersonal business culture. Perhaps these men are exceptions. They themselves seem to think so: each sets himself apart from his colleagues. Mike, for example, said, "You would never get the other merchants on the block to talk to you like this. But me, I'm an open book." Similarly, Ken thinks his talent for the personal touch gives him an edge on the impersonal managers he sees all around him, while Al contrasts his own "emotional" style with the style of his cold fish of a boss.

It may be, however, that these men are not as exceptional as either they or sociological theory would have us believe. These men describe the discrepancy between how their colleagues behave and their own ambivalent desire for something more personal. But would their neighbors recognize this yearning in them? I am not at all sure. Wanting and at the same time fearing emotional contact, these men may exaggerate their own small gestures toward each other. Their neighbors, who witness only how these men behave, not their private, ambivalent rumination, might offer a harsh assessment of Ken, Mike, or Al: "a tough, aggressive, cold man." This outward appearance may be all that men see in each other, and all that sociological investigators observe in the work culture at large.

Although Ken, Mike, Al, and Ben claim to enjoy the social exchange that work allows them, each suggests, in other places, his discomfort with relationships that become too personal. Ken, for example, is careful to distinguish genuine friendship from the tactical collegiality he practices. In a similar way, Al described his first boss: "He gave a shit whether I succeeded. Told me when I was good and chewed me out when I made mistakes. Always with real affection." But a moment later, as though embarrassed by his own sentimentality, Al continued, "I don't know if he had the brains to know a good agent from a bad one.... [He's] a good salesman, a blowhard. Heart as big as the world, probably a liver to match it. Big ideas, small capacity to follow through on them."

Ben, after describing the pleasure he takes in making personal contact with his students in the fieldwork seminar, abruptly changed his tone. "I could make my [other] course more like the fieldwork seminar.... It intrigues me, but that is exactly what I argued against. Sociology of Contemporary Culture is a garbage course ... not hard-nosed data. It's overly experiential." If these men attempt to make something more personal of their contact with colleagues and clients—and they do—they also recoil, as if embarrassed and potentially demeaned by their own overtures of affection.

Ultimately each of these men defended himself against what he experienced as a particularly humiliating rejection by going on the attack. Ken demoted his protégé; Mike wrestled the entire community through a sale that he described as "a kick in the teeth"; Al contemplated resigning from the firm and going into business for himself—and in competition with his boss. These three men played out in its purest form the cycle of attempted affiliation, humiliating rejection and aggressive self-restoration. Each made use of the formula that career culture provides. Ken exploited the denial of passion that self-in-role allows. Al and Mike retreated into the comfortable aggressiveness of career trajectory, disguising their fear of seeming weakly sentimental. Ben, who also tries to make work an occasion for affection and ends up feeling demeaned for his effort, differs only in his inability to use the defense of trajectory. Either because he is afraid of being defeated or because his own rage seems overwhelming to him, Ben never quite allows himself to express his anger. His anger is detectable; it is expressed covertly, as in his fantasies of Hitler experiments. But more often, Ben's experience is of the emotional numbness he calls "boredom," which for him accompanies his eternal, constricted niceness.

If these four men describe a core syndrome, we can now position the others in relation to them. To put the matter in its most general terms, we might say that what each of them fears, and, at times, experiences, is self-diminishment, a loss of pride and power. Putting it this way, we can now see that Bob and Lew also anticipate self-diminishment, though for different reasons. Unlike the first four men, the problem Bob and Lew face does not begin with an overture of affection and an experience of rejection. Their concern about diminishment has a different cast. Bob is sensitive to feeling coerced, while Lew worries that he is incompetent and may be unmasked at any moment. If their concern about diminishment has a different psychodynamic cast, and if, therefore, it does not include all the elements of the scene that the others enact, it still makes use of career trajectory for similar ends. Lew restores his pride and vitality through career motility. Bob, in the story he tells of his father's life, denies that he was coerced by denying the trajectory of his father's career and the personal nature of their struggle.

Finally, we can now see where Don fits into the larger pattern described by the others. Like the first four men, Don is concerned about affiliation. Unlike them, he does not fear that his overtures of friendliness will make him vulnerable. Don wants to be included but fears that if he is too demanding he will become destructive. By seeing himself as an actor in role he gets to participate without overstepping his bounds.

In each of the case histories I have tried to show the reasons these men explain themselves as they do, while at the same time pointing out the price they pay. The more detailed presentation of this point has had to proceed case by case, but perhaps we can now see the more general pattern. We begin then with trajectory and, in particular, its virtues.

The culture of careers, as I said before, establishes more than an expectation about how a man should conduct himself on the job; it provides a dramatic vehicle through which he enacts and explains his life. Trajectory is the vehicle for a particular aspect of life stories—their plot. What is a life story, and what is a plot?

By life story I mean the account that each of us tells about our own lives. It is rarely a fully rendered story: few people write their autobiographies or tell them, in any detail, to curious friends or investigators. Further, when they are asked about their lives, the stories that they tell are neither complete, consistent, nor historically accurate. Yet despite their incompleteness, their internal contradiction, and their infrequent appearance in any formal rendition, there is something almost universally recognizable about the idea of having a life story. John Kotre, who has studied the generative power of peoples' retrospective accounts, describes the evocative power that the idea of life story telling had in his interviews:

> *Story* is a trigger that nearly everyone can put a finger on. . . . Though *life story* means many things to many people, it never fails to start words flowing. . . . A woman acts bizarrely in public, and we wonder what her story is. A middle-aged man tosses a wad of paper at a wastebasket; it falls short, and he mutters something about the "story" of his life. . . . Even spoken in jest, the word *story* reaches below the surface and touches semiconscious perceptions of the pattern and meaning of a life. (Kotre 1985, 26).

Life stories answer the questions that all of us, implicitly, ask about ourselves. How far have we come? How far have we left to go? (Neugarten 1968; Bardwick 1978). Have we accomplished anything in our lives? The stories people tell about themselves provide a measure of justification. Kotre suggests that the life stories his informants tell are attempts to correct the mistakes of earlier years, or to show us the adversity they have overcome. Viederman (1983) describes his use of life story telling as a form of supportive therapy: in telling their stories, patients who have been traumatized restore their own sense of life's coherence. Butler (1963) describes the uses of reminiscence in the aged: a settling of accounts, a coming to terms. Erikson, writing in a similar vein, suggests that the sense of personal history affirms the rightness, the fittingness, of the course life has taken: "Integrity is the ego's accrued assurance of its proclivity for order and meaning. . . . It is the acceptance of one's one and only life cycle as something that had to be and that, by necessity, permitted of no substitutions" (Erikson 1950, 232).

The stories that Al, Mike, and Lew tell of their careers show us what adversity they have overcome, how they have survived and triumphed. In repeated vignettes, Lew describes how he picked himself up from some defeat, or escaped a dead end, and moved on to triumph, often passing ahead of a woman who at first seemed stronger but then fell by the wayside. Mike describes how he pushed some enterprise further and faster than everyone around him—he particularly contrasts himself with the inhibited older men around him—until he arrived at a glorious pinnacle. Al's story proceeds more in reverse. He tells us what would happen if he did not forge ahead: he would retire to insignificance. By implicit comparison, he tells us that his career has made him someone who cannot be ignored. Each of these stories, then, shows us what these men have made of themselves: Lew is vital, Al is unignorable, Mike is a conqueror. This much is the positive side of these stories—the successful things they assert about their lives.

But there is another side. These stories also deny something. This denial takes two forms, one more obvious than the other. First of all, each of these stories refers to a second player in the scene: Lew's threatening but ultimately frail women, Mike's craven older men, Al's cold-hearted (or sentimentally foolish) superiors. These counterplayers represent the threatening or unsatisfying parents of childhood. Since children identify with their parents— and not only with those features they consciously admire—these counterplayers may also represent in part what these men fear about themselves. Lew fears that he himself might become immobile. For Lew, the more conscious symbol of this paralysis is his mother, who did become house-ridden. But the symbol of enervated women in Lew's adult life now refers not only to the mother but to Lew's father (who also became trapped and "immobilized" in his marriage) and what Lew fears might happen to himself. In a similar way, the craven older men that Mike sees all around him represent not only his defensive reinvention of his violent father, but also his own fearfulness.

The second disguise lies in what we might call the imagery of movement itself. Each of these stories contains not only characters, but a characteristic quality of movement. Lew, for example, not only moves on, he moves on in a decisive, abrupt, "risky" manner. Mike not only pushes ahead of everyone, his movement continually *accelerates and gains momentum* until it is unstoppable. Bob, whose story of career trajectory concentrates upon what his father did not do, explains that not only did his father stay in touch with his roots (unlike his Icarus of an uncle), the father's career path *was not a struggle*.

The difference to which I am pointing here, between characters and quality of movement, might be compared to the parts of a sentence. The characters, the men themselves and their counterplayers, are the nouns. The action itself, moving up and moving on, is a verb. But the quality of that action, moving "riskily," or "faster and faster," is an adverbial clause. These adverbial clauses have their own significance. In Lew's case, risk refers to the adventurous person his father had once been and his mother is not. The unstoppable acceleration in Mike's experience refers back to the mounting excitement and final violence of his childhood abuse.

As we move from nouns to verbs and adverbs the symbolism becomes increasingly remote. It is easy to hear in Al's description of Spencer another version of his cold, disapproving father. It is far less obvious that the acceleration and momentum of Mike's sale, or the safe that he pushed through a brick wall, recapitulates the beatings of his childhood. This remoteness, which makes our interpretive task more difficult, provides trajectory with its tactical advantage as a defense. What we, hearing the entire account, can barely fit together is indiscernible to the men themselves. It is for this reason that trajectory offers a more thorough disguise, though not a better resolution, than the more explicit idea of dispassionateness.

This distinction between nouns and verbs, or characters and plot, can of course be overdone. Just as in a sentence it is impossible to have verbs—let alone adverbs—without the nouns that incarnate them, so these life stories cannot exist without characters. Nevertheless, we can examine the different parts of the imagery separately. More important, these men can conceal different features of their concerns in different places. If we listened only to the characters in Mike's story we would hear him triumphant everywhere. It is the action, and in particular the quality of unstoppable acceleration, that points us back to what he is most reluctant to remember, and unable to escape.

Apart from career trajectory, the other principal defense that career culture places at the disposal of men is the idea that their own behavior is not motivated by private passion but by the demands of their public role. Career culture encourages the idea that private and public life are distinct. A moment ago, I argued that the imagery of career trajectory allows men to assert something positive about their lives, something about what they have overcome or accomplished. Is there an analogous virtue in the imagery of acting in role? At first glance, we might think that there is not. Erikson, who provides the most searching discussion of the relationship between private and public self-experience, concludes that "identity" is the experience of their congruence.

> The conscious feeling of having a *personal identity* is based on two simultaneous observations: the immediate perception of one's selfsameness and continuity in time; and the simultaneous perception of the fact that others recognize one's sameness and continuity. (1946, vol. 2, 365)

> We deal with a process "located" *in the core of the individual* and yet also *in the core of his communal culture,* a process which establishes, in fact, an identity of those two identities. (1968, 22)

Erikson's description of identity would seem to cast doubt on the security Don and Ken find in the idea of acting in role. But Erikson's conception refers to an ideal of harmony, both between the individual and his social milieu, and within the individual's psyche. Where this ideal harmony does not exist, a division between private and public life may be more reassuring. For example, Erikson's overall approach to psychosocial relations assumes that there is a fit between individual needs and the opportunities that societies provide. But is this always the case? (Freud, of course, once asked if it is ever the case, but let us be more modest.) Social adaptation can demand too much, as Bob says about the politics of salesmanship, or it can offer too little, as many of these men discover about work-place collegiality.

This discrepancy between what individuals need and societies offer can evoke, in adult years, themes that originate in childhood. Don, for example, feels that as a child he was invited along by other children's parents because he was "a nice kid." We could trace the meanings of "nice" back to "not hurtful" and "not demanding." Now, as an adult, he continues the same strategy. He gets to take part (up to a point) by not allowing his private demandingness to interfere with "being available." The pattern of adult life mimics that of childhood. In each case a social opportunity—being included—depends upon suppressing something about who he is privately, "a demanding person."

There is a further point. Erikson's account of identity describes a sense of psychic harmony. Various features of what one wants, how one acts and so on are synthesized into a coherent gestalt. But this coherence is also quite likely not to occur. To pursue the example Don offers: he wants to be included, but fears that if he gets too close he will destroy. He is, therefore, decidedly ambivalent. Ken, who suffers a similar ambivalence, fears that if he gets too close he will be beaten down. The separation of private and public life allows both men to manage this internal dividedness. They get to be as close to others as they can stand in their capacity of public actors, but they also get to be distant because their private lives remain, well, private.

In different ways, then, both career trajectory and the dispassionateness of role allow these men to extend themselves. They defend themselves against what seems fearful; they seem to themselves larger, more vigorous and, in some measure, more socially engaged than they were as children. Yet, as we said all along, the other side of this story is the price that every self-illusion exacts.

First of all, to the degree that men use their careers to ward off thoughts that disturb them, their allegiance to the code of work becomes obsessive and, eventually destructive. At times, these men go beyond what work expects of them. They overreact, damaging themselves and those around them. Ken, for the most part, manages a nice balance of concern and detachment from his workers. However, when the threshold of intimacy is threatened he can become ruthless. The code of impersonality becomes his rationale for brutality. Since Ken is in a position of power, he himself does not pay the price of his own excessive self-defense. But the men toward whom he is drawn, and who then inevitably disappoint him, certainly do. Mike, on the other hand, pays the price of his self-defense directly. Mike has, several times, been consumed by his version of trajectory. "Advancement," for him, symbolizes victorious struggle, it defends him against his fear of being beaten up and humiliated. His inability to relinquish the struggle when it would have been to his advantage led to his bankruptcy, and seems to have led him to similar defeats in the past.

The second problem is that men who use their careers to banish troubling fantasy find, as in any neurotic defense, that they have erected at best a leaky bulwark. If, on one side, the defensiveness of their careers leads them to excess, on the other, it never really does allay anxiety. Ken continues to be anxious about intimacy. Lew remains worried that some acidic woman will call his bluff. Mike continues to be drawn into power struggles. Al alternates between his eternal hope for recognition and his disappointed, angry retreat to self-sufficiency. Don takes extraordinary care to insulate himself from "strain." Yet even as he sits at home, he is aware that the phone might ring, invading his carefully managed calm.

The third cost of the work neurosis is how much it excludes from conscious expression. This is a more difficult assessment to make. It is comparatively easy to recognize destructive behavior or nagging anxiety. It is much more difficult to speculate about what these men might be able to feel if they were not so rigorously vigilant. Here we must rely on the barest hints in these men's accounts of a felt absence. Toward that end, we might consider in a more systematic way an issue that has surfaced in several cases.

Many of these men describe poignantly their feeling of waiting in vain for a paternal blessing. Mike said, "I can tell him to his face that I love him for what he is—my Dad—and I can't get that through his fucking head.... He will never recognize me for what I am—his son." Ken remarked, "The thing that will always bother me as long as I live is never having had my Dad say that I have done a good job with the business. And he never will say that, to the day he croaks.... It's like that movie, 'I Never Sang for My Father.'"

The anger and disappointment these men express comes as something of a surprise. As I noted in the first chapter, a body of research suggests that by middle age most men have, at least overtly, largely come to terms with their parents. Vaillant notes the disavowal of father figures in middle age (1977); Henry (1949) describes the successful business executive as a "'man who has left home.' He feels and acts as though he were on his own, as though his emotional ties and obligations to his parents were severed."

It may simply be that the men described here form a small and unrepresentative sample. However, I am more inclined to believe that there is a difference between what men say on questionnaires or in the first hour of an interview and what they will acknowledge, sometimes only indirectly, several hours later. Ben said that he forgives his father, just as he forgives anyone who, thoughtlessly but not really maliciously, may have hurt him. "Understanding prevents me from being really angry at anyone in the world. . . . I think about Hitler, and I am sorry about what he did. . . . It's just the situation, or an accident, or just being insensitive to each other's needs. No disgrace." Ben's father might not find reconciliation, framed in this unusual analogy, altogether reassuring.

The men of this study speak of their fathers with more anger and pain than most developmental theory would anticipate. Yet many of them do say that they have reached something of an accommodation, at least in their own minds. I think that within limits we may believe them. After all, their fathers are now at least in their midsixties; some have already died. Whatever battles remain must be fought with aging antagonists. Several of these men spoke, not altogether unbelievably, of their pity for the loneliness their fathers have brought upon themselves.

However, if these aging sons have now largely exhausted their struggle with the fathers of external reality, they refight the battles of childhood and adolescence with more youthful proxies. Al, for example, claims to have reached an accord with his father, though he still describes him as a "miserable old skinflint." Nevertheless, he felt that his boss—the latest in a series of suggestively similar types—had rejected him as favorite son. In a more complicated fashion that reversed the generations, Ken refought with his protégé—and relost—the struggle of affection and humiliation of his childhood.

This much, the reenactment of old defeats with modern proxies, we have seen all along. But there is something more. Not only do these men find endless new actors to rehearse old scenes, they have brought the voice of what was once external judgment within themselves. This has the effect of rendering even their achievements empty.

For example, Al said "I have done this thing [selling real estate], proved that I am awfully good at it. . . . [But] I am living with the belief . . . that money is not a very good goal." And so he imagined moving on, "working in Chin Lee . . . writing, perhaps simply doing good deeds if you will. A committed and dedicated life . . . one of a charitable or self-sacrificing nature." This man, who has turned his aggression to such dramatic vocational success, feels unsatisfied and can only imagine justification if he sacrifices himself to the self-abnegating righteousness his parents admired. And if he did surrender ambition to live in "a speck on the map," would that satisfy? Perhaps, but his past history does not lead us to believe it. We must be struck by his preference for the artifacts of community and emotionality. He is so sensitive to feeling unappreciated that he has made himself an isolate, forever marooned on the margins of other peoples' communities. He seems caught, unable to allow himself the affection he apparently wants, yet equally unable to feel satisfied with the domineering success that has become his defense.

Not all of the men have used the aggressive solution of trajectory to distance themselves from their fathers. Ben and Bob were blocked by internal inhibition (and for Bob, external circumstance); for Don and Lew, the more immediate psychodynamic task was to ally themselves with their fathers by way of identification.

The irony is that if the violence of their fantasy has made these men less able to acknowledge their disappointment and anger, they do not really feel closer to their fathers in any supportive way than do Ken, Mike, or Al. Their fathers feel intrusive, as in Bob's case, or insufficient, as in Lew's. These men sound to us, and sometimes feel to themselves, as if they have not yet arrived. Don, for example, giggles appreciatively at the bigger boys' jokes in staff meetings, while Bob complains that he spends more time with his father than with his wife. Their bond to their fathers is not suppressed as it is among the more aggressive men, but neither is it transformed into any mature, sustaining form.

These men do not use their careers to deny the affection they feel. However, because their fantasies of aggression are uncomfortably vivid, certain options for aggressive ambitiousness have been closed to them. They too have paid a price in vocational satisfaction.

They have been unable to commit themselves to their careers. Work feels hollow to them. Ben is "mediocre" and "nice" instead of ambitious and sadistic. It is not clear whom Ben fears hurting if he allows his rage expression. His fantasies, couched in Nazi imagery, are of destroying proxies of himself. There are hints that he is bitterly angry at both parents. In any case, anger is so explosive that Ben takes care not to kill insects or cut flowers. Ambitious achievement is either sadistic, as in his Nazi experiment fantasies or the experiment of the painfully loud noise, or self-punishing, scrupulous, lonely, repetitive and anonymous. Ultimately, and no matter what the endeavor, Ben says, "I get bored."

Until recently (he may be changing now), Lew mimicked in his own career the "riskiness" he preferred to attribute to his father. But this defensive identification came at a price: Lew continually accused himself of the superficiality and ineffectuality of which he was unwilling to accuse his father. The "risky life" entailed switching from job to job; Lew acknowledged he felt unattached to any of them. "I like the show, the cream. I have spent my whole life siphoning off the cream. . . . As soon as it gets to the nitty-gritty, I'll back off." The others express a similar detachment. Bob, who gave up on ambition and settled into his father's company, wanted to retire at thirty-five. Ben fears that he already has retired. Don, who says, "I am like my father. I'm a nice guy," is not bored by work so much as overwhelmed by it. The detachment that he imposes upon himself extends beyond work. We cannot help noticing the strictness of his service-machine approach to relationships. We wonder how rich his life can be.

13

Theory as Cultural Criticism

In the last chapter I suggested that careers can be seen as theater. They offer men a stage, a script, and an audience of colleagues (an internal audience as well) for the performance of life stories. But if this is theater it is of a peculiar sort. For the point of this performance has as much to do with what is silenced as what is expressed. Careers not only render manifest an idealized version of a man's life, they also, very significantly, suppress other, more troubling self-impressions. I have tried to show the cost, measured in rigid, destructive behavior, gnawing anxiety, and emotional impoverishment, of this self-suppressing performance.

This brings me, finally and briefly, to the role of academic theory. If careers are psychosocial theater, then theory, ideally, should play the role of critic. It should hold up for our inspection the language in which we explain ourselves. In particular, it should point out the conventions by which we disguise ourselves from ourselves, the public formulas that save us—to our own greater loss—from looking at what we prefer not to see. But academic theory can only reveal the unspoken in public culture if it does not already contain the same silences within itself. Is it possible that our best established ways of studying men and their careers retain, in the very form of their inquiry, the self-diminishment that these men's explanations impose upon them?

Throughout this study I have contrasted a psychodynamic interpretation of men's careers with the explanations these men offer of themselves. In so doing, it has never been my intention to argue that psychodynamic motives are more profound, more ultimately determining, than social constraints. Just the opposite. I have tried to show how much social formulas shape psychodynamic conflict by giving expression to one of its terms while encouraging suppression of another. My effort has been to show the joint existence—the alliance—of cultural formula and private motive.

The difference between the perspective I have advanced here and that of the men themselves is that the men reduce this joint experience to a single term. The explanations they offer banish private motivation, and instead proclaim that they are simply operating in the ways good business practice requires. I have tried to show that these explanations are a form of self-deception—psychodynamically intelligible, to be sure, but costly nonetheless.

In these last pages I would like to compare the explanations men offer of themselves with two theoretical perspectives that address a similar territory: classical role theory and Eriksonian "psychosociology." In subtle ways these two perspectives repeat, at the level of theory, the simplification men make in describing themselves, and are therefore unable to appreciate men's self-deception.

In its most thoroughly sociological form, role theory provides an account of lives that deliberately dispenses with private motives. It argues that social context is all we need to know in order to understand individuals' reasonings. So, for example, Becker, toward the end of a 1964 essay entitled, "Personal change in adult life," describes a radically situationist view of the relationship between social structure and personality:

> The processes we have considered indicate that social structure creates the conditions for both change and stability in adult life. . . . They enable us to arrive at general explanations of personal development in adult life *without requiring us to posit unvarying characteristics of the person, either elements of personality or of "value structure."* (pp. 155–56, emphasis added)

In this passage, Becker makes clear the advantage he forsees in a purely sociological account of adult development. It will allow us to avoid speculating about anything that has to do with "personality" or "value structure," that is, anything not given by the social situation. Becker sees this as a welcome simplification, but he has abandoned what is most important for our purpose.

There is an interesting parallel between the advantages Becker forsees and the use to which Don, for example, puts a similar, informal theory of himself. Don uses the idea of acting "in role" to draw a boundary between his private motives and his public duties. He explains that by "shifting roles" he prevents the cares of work from intruding upon his family. Only by shifting roles, self-consciously "separating out," is he able to make himself wholly available to the multiple counterplayers in his life. We have found reason to question Don's account. There is a suggestion, though certainly not conclusive evidence, that Don is never wholly available to anyone. He is available to his family in a technical sense, he fulfills the duties of a father. But we wonder how available he makes himself emotionally.

Even if Don's various partners found his technical approach to being available wholly satisfying, we might remain disappointed by his solution. In choosing to describe himself (and, more important, to experience himself) from the perspective of acting in role, Don has taken up a point of view outside himself. He experiences himself in terms of his value to others, but renounces the legitimacy of his own private cares. This perspective diminishes him; it makes him into nothing but an eternal partner. (Don, of course, would protest. He feels that he is most fully realized as a partner. But we notice how much he pushes own concerns underground, and at what cost.)

An analogy may help illustrate the issue. Men are not alone in adopting the imagery of self-in-role. Don's comments have a great deal in common with what has become a popular image among women, and so a similar criticism may be relevant. The dilemma of women who seek careers is not simply the burden of multiple commitments upon their time and energy; it is that the domains of career and family require different combinations of aggressive competence and nurturance. The imagery of self-in-role allows women to claim—as do a host of television commercials, ever our best index of where popular self-imagery has arrived—that they can be as tough as the man in the next office from nine to five, and seductively gentle after hours. The idea of switching temperament from role to role allows women, like Don, to claim they can be all things to all partners. But is this really a liberating claim? From the dominant male perspective, women have always been viewed as partners, and have in turn so viewed themselves. The imagery of self-in-role promises them greater efficacy in this endeavor. But does it not do so at the price of reinforcing their status as nothing but counterplayers?

The similarity between role theory and the informal theory Don has about himself is in the description of motives purely in terms of public duties. Not to exaggerate the point—this explanation is partly correct, but incomplete. We all experience ourselves partly in terms of how we perform our public duties and how others judge that performance. But this experience of oneself as a public actor is not the entirety of self-experience. Don's description of himself as a man who moves from one set of public obligations to another is a substantial reduction. Whether we can observe this reduction depends upon the initial conceptual commitments we make.

From the sociological perspective, "role" is a neutral, descriptive term, no more problematic than the concept of length or color. Don's case alerts us to the idea that this is a particular way of experiencing oneself, an experience that attempts to take up an external point of self-observation and denigrates everything about private motive that does not serve social adaptation. Our ability to notice that this is a self-conception, formed out of a combination of cultural and private reasons and bearing certain costs, depends upon our recognizing the difference between public roles and the private life projects they (partially) embody. But role theory, in its purest form, abolishes this distinction before we have had a chance to study it.

An alternative to the radical simplification of pure role theory might be a social psychology that takes seriously both the skeleton of culture and the private dreams that are hung upon it. Erikson, of course, has been our principal spokesman for what such a composite perspective would include. A moment ago I quoted his definition of identity: "two simultaneous observations: the immediate perception of one's selfsameness and continuity in time; and the simultaneous perception of the fact that others recognize one's sameness...."

Erikson's repeated emphasis on the "simultaneousness" of private and public self-experience should not obscure how his view differs from role theory. Erikson lays great weight on the awareness of personal history. This awareness confirms that one is a unique individual with enduring, personal commitments. If, going further, the experience of identity finds a congruence between all that one has been (and might become) and a social niche, it nevertheless preserves the conceptual distinction between private motive and public role. This distinction is what pure role theory abolishes.

But although Erikson's perspective is, for our purpose, an improvement, there is a problem here as well. In his insistence on simultaneity, Erikson does not tell us which experience predominates. He encourages the conclusion that, in identity, the subjective experience of individuality and public role are equally salient. But this is not the story we have heard. Don does not experience himself "simultaneously" as a private person and a public actor; he has subjugated the private man to the public one. It is as if he were trying to escape the experience of his private life by fleeing into the imagined security of his public persona. Were we to construct a psychosocial account of career culture on the Eriksonian principle of giving equal weight to private and public self-experience, we would be inaccurate. The more accurate account must show how men's private experience of themselves has been submerged beneath their experience of themselves as public actors.

At first glance, this might seem to return us to Becker's position. Perhaps Erikson is wrong, perhaps all we need know to appreciate the experience of identity is the actor's public role. But no, this is not quite the case. Identity, experienced solely in terms of public role, is a diminishment of what Erikson has in mind. Erikson is speaking about an ideal of identity, and often sounds as if he imagines that ideal were contemporary reality. Role theory, in its pure sociological form, has taken the reduction of that ideal as its point of conceptual departure. It does seem to be the case that men who follow the career code view themselves as if they were nothing but public actors. But this is not a way of talking we should accept at face value. It is not a neutral fact about oneself, like one's height or age. It is a form of self-consciousness, a decision to describe selfhood in half the tones that might be available, serving the ends of psychodynamic conflict, and donated to this service by our particular culture.

Ideally, cultural criticism should enlarge public discourse. If the theater of careers obscures what we are able to acknowledge of our lives, interpretation should expose the reasons and strategies through which that obscurity operates. But interpretation can only illuminate the world through the theoretical lenses that are available to it, and neither role theory nor Eriksonian psychosociology are likely to serve this cause. "Identity" envisions no conflict, while role theory has eliminated one of the contestants.

What we need is a way of talking about the conflictual relationship between private life projects and the public formulas in which they are enacted. Individuals, and the career culture within which they operate, are all too ready to suppress one in favor of the other. It should be our task—those of us who study adult lives and the culture in which we find ourselves—to point out the reasons for and tactics of that reduction. We should be roiling the waters, refusing to tolerate the silence to which psychodynamic and cultural suppression are such ready partners. Our aim, as catalysts of social discourse, should be to raise the problem of work, and more generally of lives lived in the medium of any less-than-fulfilling cultural vehicle, to the level of public visibility and debate. How we study this territory, what conceptual choices we make, will determine our ability to comment on the silence, or find ourselves its unwitting partner.

Bibliography

Bardwick, J. M. 1978. Middle age and a sense of future. *Merrill-Palmer Quarterly*. 24:129–38.
Becker, H. 1964. Personal change in adult life. *Sociometry*. 27:40–53.
Brim, O. G. 1976. Theories of the male mid-life crisis. *The Counseling Psychologist*. 6:2–9.
Brod, H. 1987. *The making of masculinities: the new men's studies.* Winchester, Mass.: Allen & Unwin.
Butler, R. N. 1963. The life review: an interpretation of reminiscence in the aged. *Psychiatry*. 26
Campbell, A. 1981. *The sense of well-being in America: recent patterns and trends.* New York: McGraw-Hill.
Chinoy, E. 1952. The tradition of opportunity and the aspirations of automobile workers. *American Journal of Sociology*. 57:453–59.
Erikson, E. H. 1946. Ego development and historical change. *The Psychoanalytic Study of the Child*. 2:359–96.
_____. 1950. *Childhood and society.* New York: Norton.
_____. 1968. *Identity: youth and crisis.* New York: Norton.
Farrell, M. P., and Rosenberg, S. D. 1981. *Men at mid-life.* Boston: Auburn House.
Freud, S. 1922. *Beyond the pleasure principle.* London: International Psychoanalytical Press.
_____. 1962. The ego and the id. In J. Strachey (Ed.), *The standard edition of the complete psychological works of Sigmund Freud.* London: Hogarth Press.
Fried, B. 1976. *The middle age crisis.* New York: Harper & Row.
Gould, R. L. 1972. The phases of adult life: a study in developmental psychology. *American Journal of Psychiatry*. 129:521–31.
Henry, W. E. 1949. The business executive: the psychodynamics of a social role. *American Journal of Sociology*. 4:286–91.
Jaques, E. 1965. Death and the mid-life crisis. *International Journal of Psychoanalysis*. 46:502–14.
Kanter, R. M. 1977. *Men and women of the corporation.* New York: Basic Books.
Kotre, J. 1984. Outliving the self: generativity and the interpretation of lives. Baltimore: Johns Hopkins.
Kris, E. 1956. The personal myth. *Journal of the American Psychoanalytic Association*.
Lasch, C. 1979. *The culture of narcissism.* New York: W. W. Norton.
Levinson, D. J. 1976. Periods in the adult development of men: ages 18 to 45. *The Counseling Psychologist*. 6:21–25.
_____. 1978. *The seasons of a man's life.* New York: Alfred A. Knopf.
Lowenthal, M. F., et al. 1975. *Four stages of life.* San Francisco: Jossey Bass.
Mills, C. W. 1953. *White collar.* New York: Oxford University Press.
Neugarten, B. L. 1968. Adult personality: toward a psychology of the life cycle. In B. L. Neugarten (Ed.), *Middle age and aging.* Chicago: University of Chicago Press.

———. 1968. The awareness of middle age. In B. L. Neugarten (Ed.), *Middle age and aging.* Chicago: University of Chicago Press.

———. 1976. Adaptation and the life cycle. *The Counseling Psychologist.* 6:16–20.

Ochberg, R. 1986. College drop outs: the developmental logic of psychosocial moratoria. *Journal of Youth and Adolescence.* 15:4.

———. 1987. The male career code and the ideology of role. In H. Brod (Ed.), *The making of masculinities: the new men's studies.* Winchester, Mass.: Allen & Unwin.

Osherson, S. D. 1980. *Holding on or letting go.* New York: The Free Press.

Parsons, T. 1964. *Social structure and personality.* New York: The Free Press.

Riesman, D. 1950. *The lonely crowd.* New Haven: Yale University Press.

Rosenberg, S. D., and Farrell, M. P. 1976. Identity and crisis in middle aged men. *International Journal of Aging and Human Development.* 7:153–70.

Rosenwald, G. C., and Wiersma, J. 1983. Women, career changes, and the new self: an analysis of rhetoric. *Psychiatry.* 46:213–29.

Schafer, R. 1983. *Aspects of internalization.* New York: International Universities Press.

Sennet, R. 1978. *The fall of public man.* New York: Random House.

Sofer, C. 1970. *Men in mid-career.* Cambridge, Eng.: University Press.

Sutton, F. X. 1956. *The American business creed.* Cambridge, Mass.: Harvard University Press.

Tamir, L. 1982. *Men in their forties: the transition to middle age.* New York: Springer.

Taylor, C. 1979. Interpretation and the sciences of man. In P. Rabinow (Ed.), *Interpretive Social Science.* Berkeley: University of California Press.

Vaillant, G. E. 1977. *Adaptation to life.* Boston: Little, Brown.

Vaillant, G. E., and McArthur, C. C. 1972. Natural history of male psychological health. *Seminars in Psychiatry.* 4.

Viederman, M. 1983. The psychodynamic life narrative: a psychotherapeutic intervention useful in crisis situations. *Psychiatry:*46:236–46.

Index

Adolescence, 41–43, 60, 79, 107–9, 115, 120–21
Affection, denied by men, 5, 60–61, 137. *See also* Personal relationships at work
Aggression, 32, 43–45, 47, 58–59, 62, 76–77, 90, 138. *See also* Power; Humiliation
Ambition, 85–86, 93–95, 112–15. *See also* Career advancement
Ambivalence, 49, 84
American Business Creed, 7
Anger, 35, 41, 47, 128–29

Bankruptcy, 101, 110
Bardwick, J., 139
Becker, H., 148
Bordin, E., 5
Brothers, death of, 27, 29, 128; relationships with, 33–34, 35, 44–46, 77–78, 126–27, 128
Butler, R., 139

Campbell, A., 15
Career advancement, 72–74, 76, 121–22; advantage over detachment, 52–53, 140–41; expected, 9–10, 94–95; and impersonality, 10; and middle age, 57, 69; psychodynamic meaning of, 10, 57, 67–69, 79, 80, 125, 136, 138
Career culture: principal themes, 4, 6; and psychodynamic defense, 11–12, 31–32, 40, 47, 81, 116, 135, 137–38. *See also* Career advancement, Personal relationships at work
Childhood, 27–30, 40–41, 66, 77–79, 90–91, 92, 108–10
Children, 23, 24, 26, 58, 76
Chin Lee, 61, 64, 67
Chinoy, E., 9
College experience, 23, 41–42, 45, 60, 72, 84–85, 86, 89, 107
Collegiality. *See* Personal relationships at work
Community spirit, 62–63

Death: of father, 28–29, 129–31; of brother, 28–29, 30, 128; of uncle, 113
Depression, 121–22, 123, 129
Detachment: expected of men, 5, 6–7; in men's self-description, 25–26, 39–40, 47. *See also* Impartiality
Dream, 3, 13

Ego-ideal, 4
Emotion, 59, 62, 76. *See also* Aggression, Detachment
Employment, current, 23–25, 27, 33, 38–40, 58–59, 71–72, 73–74, 84, 87–88, 108–9, 119, 131–32
Employment history, 23, 25, 26–27, 43–44, 59–60, 61, 73–75, 86, 108, 119, 120–23
Erikson, E., 139, 141, 150

Families. *See* Children; Wives
Family legends, 91–92, 95, 112–17, 125–26
Farrell, M., & Rosenberg, D., 14, 15, 16
Father-in-law, 43, 46
Fathers: common themes, 136; conflicts reenacted at work, 74, 79–80; disapproving, emotionally distant, and ineffectual, 42, 64–65, 92, 126–27; idealized, 125; identification with, 127–28; paternal blessing withheld, 45–46, 78, 129–30, 143–47; resolution of conflict, 16, 92–93, 144; violent temper, 40–41, 66, 77–79, 92
Freud, S., 4
Friendship, 36

Guilt, 28

Henry, W., 10, 17
Hermeneutical circle, 19
Hitler, A., 87–89, 93
Homosexuality, 83, 122
Humiliation, 36–37, 46, 75, 77–78, 87, 94, 111

Identification, 127–28, 130
Identity: and career, 4, 141–42; theoretical critique of, 150
Impartiality, expected in men, 5, 6–7, 38, 49, 103–4
Interpretation: of cases, 19; and objectivity, 17–18; and psychoanalytic depth, 19–20
Interviews, 13–14, 24, 63, 84, 105–6, 119

Kanter, R., 9
Kotre, J., 139
Kroyt, B., 64–65

Levinson, D., 3, 4, 15
Life stories: and denial, 140; and imagery of movement, 141; and self-explanation, 139
Life structure, 3

Masculinity, 5
Memories of childhood, 28, 90–91, 109–10
Mentoring, 16, 34, 51–52, 59
Midlife crisis, 4, 15–16
Money: and emotional generosity, 43–44, 65, 66; not a sufficient goal, 9, 61
Mothers, 29, 64, 77, 114, 129; depressed and ineffectual, 123–24; emotionally distant, 65; idealized and disparaged, 76, 90

Neugarten, B., 15, 16, 139
Neurotic costs, 31–32, 80–81, 116, 128, 131, 143–45

Osherson, S., 3, 5
Outer-directed personality, 8

Personal relationships at work: with clients, colleagues and customers, 6–8, 31, 59, 85, 87, 102–3, 137; enjoyed by men, 8, 26–27, 38, 59, 76, 137; expected of men, 7–8; limits of, 9, 39–40; strain of, 8, 37, 50, 103

Power, 36–37, 74–75
Psychoanalytic theory, 17–18
Psychosomatic symptoms, 10

Riesman, D., 8
Role: and self-representation, 25, 32, 48, 50, 141; theory, critique of, 148–49; and women's movement, 149

Schafer, R., 98
Self-diminishment, 138. *See also* Humiliation; Depression
Self-doubt, 124
Self-in-role. *See* Role and self-representation
Self-representation: perfected, 3, 4, 5; self-in-relation-to-another, 98
Self-understanding, 30–31, 32, 47, 68–69, 72, 80, 94, 102, 111–12, 115–16, 127, 130, 132. *See also* Neurotic costs
Sennett, R., 8
Shakers, 62
Sisters, 29, 65, 104
Sofer, C., 9
Stress, 24–25
Supervisor-supervisee relationships, 24–25, 38–40, 58–60, 67–68
Sutton, F., 7, 8

Tamir, L., 15
Taylor, C., 18, 19
Trajectory. *See* Career advancement

Vaillant, G., 16
Viederman, M., 139

Wished-for self. *See* Self-representation, perfected
Wives, 25, 26, 106